The Southern Way

Simon Lilley and John Wenyon

The Class 71 and 74 Locomotives

Special Issue 14

www.crecy.co.uk

© 2017 Simon Lilley and John Wenyon

ISBN 9781909328648

First published in 2017 by Noodle Books

All editorial submissions to:
The Southern Way (Kevin Robertson)
Conway
Warnford Rd
Corhampton
Hants SO32 3ND
Tel: 01489 877880
editorial@thesouthernway.co.uk

All rights reserved. No part of this book may be reproduced or transmitted in any form or by any means electronic or mechanical, including photocopying, recording or by any information storage without permission from the Publisher in writing. All enquiries should be directed to the Publisher.

A CIP record for this book is available from the British Library

Publisher's note: Every effort has been made to identify and correctly attribute photographic credits. Any error that may have occurred is entirely unintentional.

Print managed in the UK by LatimerTrend

Noodle Books is an imprint of
Crécy Publishing Limited
1a Ringway Trading Estate
Shadowmoss Road
Manchester M22 5LH

www.crecy.co.uk

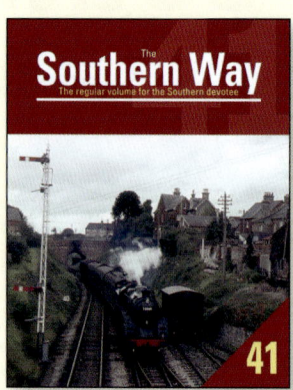

Issue No 41 of THE SOUTHERN WAY ISBN 9781909328686 will be available in January 2018 at £14.50.

To receive your copy the moment it is released, order in advance from your usual supplier, or it can be sent post-free (UK) direct from the publisher:

Crécy Publishing Ltd (Noodle Books)

1a Ringway Trading Estate, Shadowmoss Road, Manchester M22 5LH

Tel 0161 499 0024

www.crecy.co.uk

enquiries@crecy.co.uk

Front cover:
No 74001 waiting to depart from Waterloo 15 August 1976 with a boat special to Southampton Eastern Docks, conveying passengers for SS *Oriana*. *Grahame Arnold*
Class 71 No E5007 at Stewarts Lane after a recent overhaul. The locomotive was the first of the class to be painted in the new rail blue livery.
Class 47 Preservation Project Archive

Title page:
A well presented No 74007 rests at the buffer stops at Waterloo after arrival from Southampton Docks with a boat train service in the summer of 1977.
Class 47 Preservation Project Archive

Rear cover:
E5001 on display at Crewe Electric Depot Open Day in May 1997 *Class 47 Preservation Project Archive*

Contents

Introduction 4

Acknowledgements 4

1   Prelude 5

2   Design Development – The HA Electric Locomotives 7

3   Testing and Commissioning 21

4   The 1960s 26

5   Livery Changes 42

Eastleigh Works 46

6   Modifications 48

7   The HB Electro-Diesels – Origins 55

8   The HBs' Arrival on the Southern Region and into Service 68

9   Class 74 Technical Problems 74

10   The 1970s 82

Waterloo 94

11   The Final Years and Withdrawal 1976-1977 96

The Farewell Tour 107

12   Preservation 109

Conclusion 112

Appendix 1
Locomotive History 113

Appendix 2
Main technical Dimensions 114

Bibliography 115

Index 116

Introduction

This book is a companion volume to the *Southern Way Special Issue 11 The 'Booster' Locos CC1/CC2/20003* published in April 2016.

It is the first detailed study of the life and work of the Class 71 electric locomotives, and the Class 74 electro-diesels. Both types were conceived as replacements for steam traction, and in both cases their service lives were far shorter than envisaged originally.

Through detailed research of original archive documentation and other previously unpublished material, we are able to shed new light on many key aspects of both classes history. We look in detail at the reasons why the Class 71s were delivered late to the Southern Region and the effects on both phases of the Kent Coast electrification scheme.

For the first time we have been able to piece together the reasons behind the Southern Region's decision to convert existing locomotives for the Bournemouth electrification scheme rather than build new ones as planned originally. New light is also shed on the little known proposal that the new large electro-diesel locomotive design for the scheme would have incorporated extensive use of Glass Reinforced Plastic.

We also look at the modifications, large and small, made to both types over the years showing how the two classes evolved during their relatively short periods in service.

Acknowledgements

The production of this book would not have been possible without the help of many others. We would like to thank the staff at the National Archives at Kew, the Institution of Mechanical Engineers Library, the National Railway Museum in York, for their help during the researching of this book and allowing access to No E5001, the staff at Barrow Hill, Paxman historian Richard Carr, Dennis Hoy for making so much technical information on the Class 74s available to us, and Paul Rowntree. We would also like to acknowledge the help of the Class 47 Preservation Project Archive and Grahame Arnold for the use of a number of photographs from their respective collections. Finally, we must thank our families for their patience and support during the writing of this book. Without all of these people, it would have been so much harder to research, write and illustrate.

Simon Lilley
John Wenyon

1
Prelude

The last of the three Co-Co locomotives, No 20003, was completed in September 1948. The trio proved useful mixed-traffic locomotives and demonstrated the booster system's capabilities and worth, so paving the way for the smaller, but more powerful HA locomotives.
Class 47 Preservation Project Archive

The origins of both the Class 71s and indeed the Class 74s lie in a report produced in May 1944 by the Southern Railway's Chief Electrical Engineer (CEE), Alfred Raworth, entitled *Proposed Extensions of Electrification*. He projected electrifying all the company's routes to the east of, and including, the line between Basingstoke and Southampton. The real advantage of electrification was in the reduced operating costs. His calculations showed operating costs of £2,799,099. This compared to £1,555,185 if electric traction was used. The number of train miles under electric traction were reduced as it was believed 'assisting required' mileage would not be required as the electric locomotives would be sufficiently powerful to handle all trains unassisted. Locomotive coal trains would be eliminated, with the movement of coal wagons and dead engines reduced by 90%.

The use of electric traction would enable a significant increase in overall speeds when compared to the steam locomotives then in use. He quoted the example of a Victoria to Ramsgate service with nine intermediate stops: under steam, the journey time was 2 hours 13 minutes, this would be cut to 1 hour 53 minutes by using electric traction.

Raworth's report also examined the feasibility of using 1500v DC overhead electrification instead of the existing third rail system. Based on the information available at the time, Raworth saw the overhead system as being prohibitively expensive to install. Furthermore, when the LBSCR had used overhead wires, the maintenance costs were six times greater than the third rail system that in time replaced them. Future schemes, he decided, would continue to use the third rail system.

On 24 October 1946, the Southern Railway Board considered Raworth's report along with one prepared following a fact finding visit to the United States of America and Canada made the previous June. The delegation's report published on 20 September contained three main recommendations. Firstly, that high density lines should be electrified with priority related to the proportion of steam mileage over lines already electrified. Secondly, multiple-units should be used for passenger work and electric locomotives for trunk freight working between and only calling at electrified departure and arrival sidings of yards. The final recommendation was that diesel traction should be used in non-electrified areas, marshalling and yard shunting, and for pick up freight services.

The board decided that approval in principle would be given to a wide ranging electrification scheme. The following routes were to be electrified: Gillingham to Ramsgate and Dover, Sevenoaks to Dover, Maidstone East to Ashford, Tonbridge to Hastings and finally South Croydon to Horsted Keynes. The following week on 31 October, the Southern Railway held a press conference chaired by Eustace Missenden to announce this £15 million scheme. The company anticipated that subject to available materials and labour, the scheme could be completed by 1955.

Had Alfred Raworth's 1944 plan come to fruition, the Southern Railway would have needed to build a number of electric locomotives to meet its various needs. Some mainline services would have utilised Booster locomotives of which two were already in service. Whilst the third Booster locomotive, No 20003, was still under construction, serious consideration was given to the building of a fourth locomotive. This debate went on for a number of years before being overtaken eventually by the planning work for the Kent Coast electrification in the mid-1950s.

Shortly after nationalisation, the fourth locomotive issue was discussed at a meeting held at Waterloo on 20 February 1948. Amongst those present was John Elliot the Chief Regional Officer (CRO), the Chief Mechanical Engineer (CME) O. V. S. Bulleid together with his assistant Lionel Lynes, and the Chief Electrical Engineer C. M. Cock and his assistant. The meeting's main purpose was to consider non-steam locomotives, and discussed at the meeting were the region's three electric locomotives. The minutes recorded that 'English Electric had contacted the Southern Region saying that they had a complete spare set of electrical equipment of the type recently used in the construction of electric locomotive No 20003'. The Superintendent of Operations (SoO), S. W. Smart, judging by the minutes, was very keen to pursue the idea of a fourth electric locomotive, referred to incidentally as No CC4. Smart went so far as to ask for this to be authorised. O. V. S. Bulleid commented, though, that it would take 18 months to prepare the mechanical equipment.

The next documented step in the fourth locomotive story came from a surprising direction. On 15 September 1949, the Drawing Office at Doncaster produced an outline design for the Southern Region of a 2,500hp Co-Co electric locomotive. The body design was similar to No 20003, but instead of its flat 4SUB-style cab front, Doncaster had included a nose where equipment including the equipment frames and exhausters would have been located. As with the three locomotives already in service, this design would have utilised two sets of booster equipment. Numbered No 20101 on the drawing, the locomotive would have been 63ft long and 8ft 8¼in wide.

This work continued, and Doncaster produced a second drawing dated 6 January 1950. This was to the same basic design as that from the previous September although the bodyside ventilator arrangement was revised. Some additional detail was now included. The locomotive's total weight was given as 126 tons, an axle weight of 21 tons per axle. The other main dimensions remained unchanged.

The issue, however, did not completely fade away. *The British Railways – Southern Region Mechanical & Electrical Engineer's Department Electric Traction Section Rolling Stock Technical Section Report* for 1950 published on 16 February 1951 provides a further insight into the region's thinking at the time. In the section headed 'Other Developments' the construction of a fourth electric locomotive was discussed. An outline schedule prepared by the Operating Department was considered to justify construction, as equipment for it already existed. An increase in the number of locomotives would reduce the per unit maintenance cost and the heavy development costs attributed to No 20003 could then be spread over to a fourth locomotive.

By the autumn of 1953 the thinking of the Southern Region's Chief Mechanical and Electrical Engineer (CM&EE) H. H. Swift was clearly moving away from a Co-Co locomotive and towards a Bo-Bo locomotive instead. On 17 October 1953 in a memorandum headed 'Locomotives for the Eastern Electrification' (the Kent Coast Scheme) he wrote that two basic locomotive types would be required, one a 1,000hp plus Bo-Bo diesel-electric and the other a 2,500hp booster electric locomotive.

The basic technical specification he set out for the electric locomotive was for a single booster machine of between 2,500 and 3,000hp fitted with electric train heating only. Swift went on to say that a locomotive conforming to this outline specification could probably be built as a Bo-Bo type with a weight of around 80 tons. This would of course be the cheapest arrangement, but because of the need to haul loose-coupled freight trains, such a locomotive would probably have to be a Co-Co type weighing 100 tons, simply for braking purposes.

One of the last references to a possible Co-Co locomotive is on 29 October 1953 when Swift wrote to English Electric. He asked them to design an electric locomotive for when the Eastern electrification is authorised. He said that he was keen that these locomotives should be physically smaller and cheaper than the 2,500hp locomotive originally proposed back in 1949 by Doncaster. He now had in mind a locomotive that would have only one booster set, no train heating boiler, and should be capable of being built as an 80-ton Bo-Bo locomotive of about 50 feet in length. With only one booster set, no train heating boiler, and therefore no 300-gallon water tank, considerable weight savings were possible. Thus, the Co-Co booster electric locomotive concept by 1953 to all intents and purposes had been superseded by a design that would become ultimately the HA Bo-Bo type. Raworth's vision of several hundred Co-Co booster locomotives would never be fulfilled and instead a much smaller number of lighter but more powerful locomotives would be built.

Given this state of affairs, it is surprising to see that the Co-Co concept should make one last 'appearance'. The Brighton Drawing Register shows that on 29 August 1956, drawing No 11771 was prepared entitled 'Proposed Weight Diagram 2,500hp Co-Co Locomotive'. This was somewhat strange, given that at the time work was already underway designing the 80-ton Bo-Bo locomotives that would become the HA type.

2
Design Development
The HA Electric Locomotives

The Kent Coast electrification scheme was one of several detailed in the British Transport Commission's (BTC) *Modernisation and Re-Equipment of British Railways* plan published in December 1954. It proposed that all of the main Southern Region routes east of a line drawn from Reading to Portsmouth would be electrified. This would extend the existing electrification in Kent to the coast taking in Ramsgate, Dover and Folkestone and on to Hastings via Ashford.

The scheme's initial planning process identified a need for 24 electric locomotives. Of these, 20 would be in traffic at any given time, with the remaining four standing spare or undergoing maintenance. A document dated 27 June 1955 entitled 'Locomotive Requirements for Kent Coast Electrification Stage 1' said 'the *Golden Arrow* and *Night Ferry*, some van and freight services will be operated by electric locomotives. These locomotives will be fitted for both conductor rail and overhead collection, so that they may work in sidings where only overhead lines are permissible'. A brief outline specification of these electric locomotives was provided. They were described as being similar in principle to existing electric locomotives, but of the latest design with a Bo-Bo wheel arrangement weighing 80 tons. It was assumed that in all cases train heating would be by direct electrical feed.

As early as October 1955, almost a year before any locomotive orders were placed, consideration was being given to some possible design aspects. On 23 October 1955, S. B. Warder, now the BTC's Chief Electrical Engineer, wrote to the Southern Region's General Manager C. P. Hopkins, suggesting a meeting. Warder said he had some thoughts on the locomotives' frontal appearance and wanted to see how practical his ideas were.

One consequence of the Kent Coast scheme was the need to decide on the train heating system to be used. For the multiple-unit worked services, this would be electric using the third-rail supply as the source. For the locomotive-hauled services, whilst electric heating was the preferred choice, some planning and potential modification to stock would be required. This was an issue Mr Hopkins raised with the Carriage & Wagon Engineer at Eastleigh Mr R. B. Illston, in early December 1955. The main issue to resolve, Hopkins said, was the electrical supply from both diesel and electric locomotives for carriage warming. Mr Illston replied on 31 December saying that providing the supply issues were settled within six months, he did not anticipate any difficulty in equipping the region's steam-heated stock with electric train heating in the time proposed. He assumed the current supply from either a diesel or electric locomotive would be the same. Separate arrangements would have to be made with SNCF, the Pullman Car Co Ltd, and other regions to equip their stock allocated to run over the Southern Region's electrified network, with suitable electric heaters. He was seeking information from the Chief Operating Superintendent about such stock in order to study the problem in detail.

Above: **The model locomotive produced in early 1956, showing the first thoughts as to what the electric locomotives for the Kent coast electrification scheme might look like. The model is now displayed at the National Railway Museum's Warehouse.** *Jane Lilley*

At the BTC's request, the Southern Region designed the locomotives' mechanical parts at Brighton under the guidance of the Mechanical Engineer (Design) R. G. Jarvis. The Brighton Drawing Register shows that the design work began on 9 January 1956 with the production of drawing No 11583 which was the proposed basic outline arrangement of the new type. The planned locomotive weighed 80 tons and was 50ft long over the buffers. Prepared at the same time, was a further drawing No 11584, which showed the proposed layout of the end fittings.

The BTC and the Southern Region met on 30 January 1956 to look at design matters in detail. At the meeting, the drawings produced three weeks earlier and a model were studied at length and a number of options discussed. Consideration was given to whether a 'nose' was needed. With the need to keep the weight at 80 tons, and there being no equipment that logically could be located there, it was agreed that one was not required. Other issues under discussion were the use of marker lights in place of the discs as seen on the drawing and model and also a possible livery. On this last point, Christian Barman, the BTC's Publicity Officer, would be the point of contact between the Commission and the Southern Region, especially as the BTC were soon to make some general policy decisions on diesel and electric locomotive liveries.

The design work progressed quickly. By 6 March, H. H. Swift was able to send Christian Barman some initial drawings. One was of the end elevation, along with a sketch showing the driving compartment and the driving position in relation to the floor, the seat, controls and window.

The next major design phase started at Brighton concentrated on the bogies. On 19 April work began on three different potential designs, described in the register as 'Swiss', 'French' and 'Pennsylvania'.

All of the regional CM&EEs, along with R. C. Bond, the BTC's CME, and S. B. Warder, the BTC's CEE, met on 16 April at the Euston Hotel. Their aim was to finalise the 1958 Locomotive Building programme, of which the Southern Region's electric locomotives would be a part. The meeting noted that the detailed design work was already underway, being done by the Southern Region on behalf of the BTC. It was proposed to manufacture the mechanical parts in railway workshops, though no decision had been made yet as to where. In late 1956, R. C. Bond allocated this work, including construction of the locomotives themselves, to Doncaster.

The three bogie design options were narrowed down to two by the early summer. On 8 June, two new drawings were started, one for a proposed bogie, the other for a proposed bogie 'Pennsylvania type'. The same day saw the first proposed equipment layout drawing. These were soon followed by the proposed frame drawing on 11 June and a proposed locomotive weight diagram on 15 June.

Somewhat curiously, Brighton started work on 20 July on a schematic diagram of pipes from the boiler. All the discussions the Southern Region had had to date on the new locomotives' train heating supply had centred on it being electric rather than steam. Given the compact nature of the proposed locomotives, it is difficult to see where a steam heating boiler and the associated water tanks could have been located.

The BTC approved the Kent Coast Electrification scheme on 27 September 1956. The initial order placed was for 13 locomotives, to be built at a total cost of £713,765. In their submission, the Southern Region said that the locomotives' planned booked passenger mileage was estimated at 126,000 per year and the annual freight mileage at 631,000.

The fine details relating to the body design and styling were completed by Professor Misha Black of the consultants Design Research Unit Ltd. Professor Black is best known for his work on several of the Western Region diesel-hydraulic types. On 10 September Mr M. G. Burrows from the Southern Region's CM&EE department sent him the model of the locomotive and some drawings. Mr Burrows suggested they should meet to discuss the locomotives' design further.

Collaboration was such that Professor Black was able to give Christian Barman a progress update on 1 November. Black said he had met with Mr Burrows and they had reached agreement on the locomotive's shape. Black continued saying that he was preparing a model based on what had been decided which should be ready in about three weeks' time.

During both phases of the Kent Coast Electrification scheme the Southern Region managed the project by way of the regular Electrification Committee meetings. These

The outer body panels were held in place by these metal straps. Mischa Black, who had been involved in the locomotives' styling, expressed concerned as to the straps' appearance. *Simon Lilley*

The main equipment compartment looking from the No 1 end. To the right the bodyside construction method can be seen, whilst to the left are the main equipment cupboards including the HT Cupboard, Current Limiter and Contactor Cupboards. Beyond them is the booster generator set. *Jane Lilley*

minutes, starting in 1956, provide us with almost a running commentary of progress and indeed the issues and problems being encountered. A number of key regional officials attended these meetings including the CM&EE and SoO.

One of the first of these took place on 3 November 1956. At that meeting Mr Sykes said that the detailed bogie design work was progressing well. He added that discussions had been held with both English Electric Co Ltd regarding electrical equipment and with Swiss Locomotive & Manufacturing Co Ltd (SLM) on licences for the flexible drive for the bogies. By January 1957 a draft contract had been received from SLM Ltd which had been commented on and passed to the BTC. They too had made comments and these had all been passed back to SLM Ltd.

The BTC Design Panel's half yearly report dated 18 July 1957, commented on the design work's progress to date. The region had been working closely with Professor Black and a full-size mock-up of the locomotive front and driver's cab had now been built. This would be used to consult with staff. The design now incorporated a roller blind headcode, rather than marker lights which were being abolished. The rate of progress was not surprising; every drawing started by the Brighton Drawing Office between 8 October 1956 and 21 October 1957 was connected to these locomotives in some way.

By the time of the Electrification Committee's meeting on 8 August 1957, the region was very clear as to their delivery programme for this first batch of 13 locomotives. They required the first two locomotives to be delivered in time to be brought into service in October 1958, with the remainder delivered in time for them to be brought into service by June 1959. A meeting was held on 14 August with the Doncaster works' management where they were advised of these requirements. The initial construction programme offered to the Southern showed the first locomotive to be delivered in August 1958, with the other 12 locomotives to be delivered at a rate of one per month thereafter.

On the design side there were still issues to be resolved. In a letter from Misha Black to Sykes on 21 August, Black said he had recently visited the design team in Brighton and whilst progress was made some issues were still outstanding, in particular the detailed design of the cab steps and the overall shape of the cab front. Black suggested setting up periodic meetings between the two parties so these outstanding items could be resolved quickly.

The following month saw further design issues identified. Writing to the Southern Region's CM&EE's department on 9 October Misha Black said he was not in favour of splitting the louvres on one side halfway down so as to make space for the lining. Indeed, he even suggested that the lining should be omitted on that side, on the grounds that no one would be able to see both sides of the locomotive at any one time. As for the positioning of the lining and the BR crest, he wanted to wait until the first locomotive was complete before making a decision. His reasoning was that it was an easier decision to make with an actual locomotive to work with. After discussion between Black and the BTC's Head of Design George Williams, it was decided that the lining would remain on both sides, though Black said he found the louvre arrangement 'oppressive'. The other issue concerning him was the arrangement of a proposed gutter over the driving window and how that could be incorporated into the cab design.

The Electrification Committee at its meeting on 17 October discussed the schedule offered by Doncaster and agreed it was unacceptable. Mr Sykes the CM&EE was instructed to discuss the problem further with his Eastern Region counterpart Mr K. J. Cook in order to resolve the matter. The two regions met on 22 October, the Southern restating their requirements with the Eastern Region responding that it might be possible for the first locomotive to be completed by May 1958, and to have all 13 locomotives delivered by May 1959 at the rate of one per month.

Further production difficulties were encountered, which the Electrification Committee were advised of at their meeting held on 8 May 1958. Whilst Doncaster works was endeavouring to meet the Southern Region's programme, the first locomotive would not be completed that month, in fact August was now the date advised. However, they did say that all 13 locomotives would now be delivered by May 1959.

Locomotive production though was not the only aspect of the project to suffer delays. At the next meeting of the Electrification Committee held on 12 June, members were appraised of difficulties with some of the project's civil engineering works, most notably at Blackheath and Herne Hill. In both cases, the work involved would not be completed by the October 1958 target date, so creating a real risk of locomotives having no work to do. The meeting also heard that if locomotive deliveries could not be accelerated from what was promised there would be motive power issues with the changeover from steam to electric traction.

Locomotive deliveries continued to be a major discussion point at many of the subsequent Electrification Committee meetings. At the 10 July meeting, attendees were told that if the current schedule was adhered to with the first electric locomotive delivered in August and then one per month thereafter, it would mean only nine, or maybe ten locomotives at most, would be delivered by the start of the new electric timetable in June 1959. Messrs Sykes and Fitch were asked to contact the Eastern Region's management to see if the delivery schedule could be improved. They wrote on 14 July asking just this. The reply from Doncaster dated 28 July said there was little that could be done to improve the situation, and that the matter would have to be raised at departmental level to effect any change.

The locomotive construction delays naturally had a knock-on effect on the planned driver training. This needed to start in October 1958 to ensure there was enough qualified staff in time for the changeover in June 1959. Mr Sykes told the 14 August meeting that in addition to the ongoing problems of late locomotive deliveries, there were also problems in recruiting suitable Instructors to deliver the driver training. The vacancies had been advertised, but only as temporary posts and as such were unattractive to many suitably qualified staff.

Mr Sykes wrote to the General Manager C. P. Hopkins on 10 September to update him on the locomotive situation. Mr Cook's estimate for delivering the first locomotive from Doncaster, Sykes said, was 'October/November 1958'. This date has been underlined in green ink with the comment 'presumably = 30 November'.

The situation if anything had worsened by the time of the next Electrification Committee meeting on 11 September. Two locomotives had been required to be in service by October 1958, and now not even the first one was likely to appear until November with deliveries at a rate of one per month after that. This would mean a maximum of only eight locomotives available by the time of the planned start of Phase One in June 1959. With no available locomotives, driver training could not start in October as planned, with the consequent problems caused for the changeover of motive power as there would be potentially insufficient numbers of trained drivers. On a more positive note, Mr Sykes reported that one Instructor vacancy had now been filled, whilst the other two positions had been re-advertised.

The locomotive situation was discussed again at the meeting held on 9 October. Now only a maximum of eight locomotives could be delivered in time. Progress though was being made regarding the recruitment of Instructors. This was being mitigated by the use of technical staff instead of recruiting Instructors. By the time of the meeting held on 13 November, there was still no sign of a locomotive being handed over from Doncaster. This meant that only a maximum of seven locomotives could be delivered in time. The training programme had been adapted to take account of these problems, but even so there was every likelihood of there being insufficient number of qualified drivers in place in time. This could mean steam traction having to be retained for longer than planned originally. The meeting also heard, there were now two of the three Instructors in post, and the 11 locomotives required for the Phase Two scheme had been included in the 1960 Locomotive Building Programme which was now awaiting BTC approval.

The last meeting of 1958 was held on 11 December. Again members heard that there was no firm date for the delivery of the first locomotive. This latest delay would mean that only six of the 13 required locomotives would be available on time. BTC approval for the second order of 11 was also still awaited. Finally, though, there was some good news when, on 31 December, the first locomotive No E5000 was delivered. The same day the Brighton Drawing Office prepared the General Arrangement drawing for the class.

Construction

The 24 locomotives were built at Doncaster. The underframe was a fabricated structure consisting of two closely spaced longitudinal members, located on each side of the locomotive's centre line. At each end was a dragbox assembly and two main cross-members at the bogie centre line. The battery box brackets were cantilevered out from the main longitudinals. Light channel-section members independent of the main underframe over their middle portion acted as both supports and bottom stiffeners for the bodysides. The flat top of the underframe was covered by 1/8in steel plates. These were continuously welded into place to provide a dust-tight underfloor seal.

The body was non stress-bearing, consisting of a central equipment compartment with a cab at each end. This central section was a metal framework with a sheet steel outer covering. The roof was divided into three sections, and the outer two sections were removable. This allowed equipment to be lifted out. The central roof section contained a well for the pantograph.

Internally, the whole body had a false floor, providing space for the cables and pipework. In the equipment compartment aluminium treadplate was used as the floor covering. On one side of the compartment was a gangway. The bodyside on that side had two small louvres set into it along with a large droplight window placed centrally. On the non-gangway side were the air intakes for the booster, traction motor blower, and the booster starting resistors.

This central compartment contained the motor-generator booster set, which comprised of the booster motor, booster generator, and the overhung auxiliary generator. There were two electrical control equipment frames, one at each end of the compartment. The larger of the two, located at the number one end, housed the main line-breaker and current limiter, booster notching camshaft, resistance starting and traction motor contactors, the reverser and field tap switch for the number one and two traction motors, and associated relays. A small control panel for the line voltage fuses and switches was also at the number one end. A smaller frame was located at the number two end. This contained the booster field regulating camshaft, resistances, and associated relays along with the reverser and field tap switch for traction motors three and four. Both frames were encased completely by dust-tight removable panels and doors.

The Cabs

The cabs comprised of a framework covered by a double skin. The outer covering was mild-steel sheet lined with asbestos and welded at all the joints. The inner skin was made from hardboard and plywood covered by cream-coloured plastic panels. The cab front comprised of two double-glazed windscreens made from ¾in toughened glass. In between, was the single glazed two-digit route indicator, lit by four bulbs. Below the windscreens was a horizontal handrail which wrapped around the front as far as the entrance door at the side. Below the handrail on the cab front were two lamp irons

The maker's plate as fitted to No E5001. *Jane Lilley*

and a footstep. The side of each cab had a full drop window. On the cab roof at each end was a ventilator and behind that a horizontally mounted whistle. An oval builder's plate made from brass and then chromed 10½in by 6in was attached below the driver's window. It read *'BUILT BY BRITISH RAILWAYS DONCASTER 1959 POWER EQUIPMENT BY ENGLISH ELECTRIC COMPANY LTD'*.

Internally, the driver's position was on the left-hand side, with an adjustable tip-up seat. The seat back was fixed to the cab's back wall. On the right-hand side a simple tip-up seat was provided for the second member of the train crew. In front of the driver's position were the master controller and brake valves along with a sloping instrument panel with the air pressure and vacuum gauges, and the speedometer. To the driver's left, mounted on the cab window pillar was the lever for the roof mounted whistle. The operating wire ran from here across the ceiling to the whistle. On the right-hand side, were the handbrake wheel and a simplified controller and brake valve. This meant the locomotive could be driven from that side when shunting. The cab floor consisted of wood planks covered with linoleum. Under the seats were electric heaters and a ceiling mounted air extractor was provided. A two-level Deadman's pedal was provided in a recess in the desk, meaning the locomotive could be driven either standing up or sat down.

Equipment

Bogies and Shoe Gear

The bogie design was a completely new one, based on a design from Swiss Locomotive Manufacturing Co Ltd. Negotiations for the necessary licences began in September 1956 and agreement was reached the following year.

The bogie frame was a box-girder type. The locomotive body was supported on a swing bolster, located longitudinally by horizontal traction links which connected it to the bogie frame itself. Two pads had spherical seats on their upper surface whilst the flat lower surface was fitted with friction pads which were arranged to slide on wearing plates on top of the bolster when the bogie rotated. The bolster ends bear on the centre buckles of the two inverted five-foot-long laminated springs, which formed the secondary suspension. These were placed at the maximum practicable distance apart to limit any tendency for the locomotive body to roll. Rubber stops were used to limit any lateral movement by the bolster to 1½in. In service, unpredictable variations in friction between the laminations of this spring produced adverse effects on the locomotive riding. Alternative forms of suspension were later

Above: **A close up of the HA type bogie.** *Simon Lilley*

Left: **The individual short plank shoe gear for third-rail current collection. At present removed from No E5001 and stored inside the locomotive.** *Simon Lilley*

considered, but not fitted until the conversion of some of the locomotives to HB electro-diesels.

The wheelsets were fitted with either Timken or SKF roller bearings from new. The roller bearings had pillar-type axlebox guides and coil primary springs. A cabled return circuit was provided which brought the return current to 55.5mm diameter copper-carbon brushes. These bore onto machined copper-clad tracks on each driving wheel centre with two brushes per wheel. This gave a return path for the traction current to the running rail ensuring the minimum amount of current as possible was transmitted through the roller bearings.

The English Electric EE532 traction motors were fully suspended. To ensure the gear wheel and pinion were meshed continuously; a certain level of flexibility was required in the drive between the armature shaft and the axle. This allowed for the vertical movement of the axle when the locomotive was in motion. To achieve this, a Brown-Boveri spring drive, made under licence by SLM, was used. A pinion was fitted to the motor armature shaft. This pinion meshed with a gear wheel running on a double-row roller bearing that was carried on a stub quill surrounding the axle and was attached to the traction motor frame.

Torque was transmitted from the pinion onto the gear wheel rim. The gear wheel contained the flexible parts in machined pockets. These flexible parts comprised of two spring cups and contained two concentric steel springs. Torque was transmitted onwards from the gear wheel to the spring cups, through the springs, to two further spring cups placed directly opposite. The springs were compressed by the torque and the spring cup was clear of the gear wheel shoulders, and in contact with the drive spider pressed onto the road wheel. The drive spider transmitted the torque to the wheels.

The arrangement's various flexible parts allowed some axle movement meaning the drive springs were part of the locomotive's suspension. A consequence of this was that some of the drive springs would be compressed when a traction motor was being removed and made it difficult to remove the bolts holding the stub quill to the bogie frame. This design was the first electric locomotive application in the UK of fully springborne traction motors.

Eight brake cylinders, one for each brake block, were fitted, minimising the brake rigging. Each cylinder had a built in slack adjuster so ensuring continued uniform brake performance. The Brake Cylinder Pressure Gauge in the cab took readings from the No 1 bogie.

Third-rail current collection was through eight standard radial-type collector shoes mounted on wooden planks and secured to the bogies by brackets at each wheelset. The location of the long laminated bogie secondary spring gave insufficient room for a 'standard' shoe beam to be fitted hence the individual short planks were used.

On each corner of the bogie was a sandbox, operated from the drivers cab.

Pantograph

As with the Southern Railway Co-Co locomotives before, the HA locomotives were provided with a roof-mounted pantograph. This was located in a well in the centre of the locomotive. It was a box-type spring raised, air operated device. If there was insufficient air in the system it could be

A basic tramway style catenary system was provided in a number of goods yards. Current collection from this system was via a box pantograph roof mounted in a central recessed well. Class 47 Preservation Project Archive

raised using a foot pump. This was located on the floor close to the Booster Motor air intake. The training material provided to footplate staff as part of their tuition, stated that between 12 and 15 strokes of the pump would be sufficient to raise the pantograph. The maximum permitted speed when taking current via the pantograph was 15mph. The normal wire height was 16ft rising gradually to 22ft at the termination points. An overlap section of conductor rail and overhead wire was provided at each location.

Train Heating Equipment

From new the HA type were equipped with Electric Train Heating (ETH). This was capable of being used on stock fitted with either the BR or UIC/SR heating systems. Initially the jumper cable was mounted on the cab front, but after a very short time in service it was relocated to a position on the bufferbeam behind the driver's side buffer.

The power for train heating was supplied from the conductor rail, through a 1kA contactor, and controlled by way of a two-way switch located in a control box on the back wall of each cab. To protect the circuits, an overload relay was fitted. If there were an overload on the train-heating circuits, the overload relay operated to open the heating contactor. At this point the heating supply was cut and would only restart when the relay was reset manually.

Connection to the train was via the positive train heating jumper cable on the locomotive, connections to and from the locomotive depended on whether BR or UIC stock was being heated. Some of the Southern Region's stock was fitted with UIC compatible equipment. When providing heat on the UIC/SR system only the locomotive plug was used so providing a single-pole heating supply. The coach plug was not to be connected to the locomotive. The coach plug would only be connected when heating stock from other regions, so providing dual-pole heating. Driving Instructions for the class issued by the Southern Region in 1961 state clearly 'train heating from these locomotives should be on the UIC/SR system using the locomotive PLUG only to provide a single-pole heating supply'.

The Brake Equipment

The Oerlikon brake equipment had two systems. The first was a straight air (non-automatic) locomotive brake. This was used when the locomotive was running light or hauling unfitted stock. Secondly, there was a fully automatic air brake for working trains of air-braked stock. The system also had proportional control for when hauling vacuum-braked stock. When built, the straight air locomotive brake had no Deadman protection and would not fail safe.

Two exhausters were provided. The 'line exhauster' was fed from the third-rail supply and ran continuously to maintain vacuum. The other exhauster, powered from the battery supply, was used to assist the 'line' exhauster when brake releasing and ensured vacuum was maintained during breaks in the power supply from the conductor rail. This 'battery' exhauster would only cut in when the locomotive ran over a fairly long gap in the supply. At that point, the booster-generator speed would fall to a point where there was insufficient voltage to drive the 'line' exhauster at a speed sufficient enough to maintain the train pipe vacuum. With the 'battery' exhauster cutting in, there was always sufficient voltage to prevent a significant drop in the train pipe vacuum.

Traction Motors

The traction motors used on the HAs were the English Electric type EE532. This motor was a six-pole, series wound, reversible, direct current machine. The armature rotated in two grease-lubricated roller bearings. At the commutator end, the motor was fitted with a double roller thrust bearing. This was to absorb the axial forces that the single helical driving pinion created on the armature shaft.

The motor's one-hour rating was 705 amps at 675 volts, 476kW-1904kW. This equated in total to 2552hp. The continuous rating was 430kW and this was developed in weak field at 69.6mph with a corresponding total locomotive tractive effort of 12,500lb.

The locomotives' Maximum Tractive Effort was limited to 43,000lb, by the setting of the overload relay. This was equivalent to 25% of the as built locomotive weight of 77 tons, and therefore 25% of its weight for adhesion.

The motors were cooled used forced ventilation. The air entered through a flanged inlet in the motor frame and exited through several openings at the 'pinion' end of the motor. Access to the commutators and brushgear was via two covers, one upper and one lower. The brushgear itself was mounted on a brush rocker ring. The location of this was pre-set, marked, and locked in place by bolted clamps during the testing phase of the manufacturing process.

The Booster Equipment

The booster control system was an updated version of that used on the earlier Southern Railway Co-Co locomotives. This meant four motors, rather than three per booster set as fitted to the Co-Co locomotives. They were placed neatly in two parallel pairs electrically either side of the booster set.

When developing the booster equipment, Dennis Lightband, the Chief Traction Machine Designer at English Electric Co Ltd, based at Bradford, opted to use the Type 831 generator which had been developed for the prototype 3,300hp diesel-electric locomotive *Deltic* as the basis for the main electrical machines of the new booster sets. They were, he determined, of a suitable frame size and power rating for the new application.

The booster set comprised of two separate pieces of equipment, Firstly, a Booster Generator which was a direct current machine and coupled to the second item the Booster

The heartbeat of the HA locomotives, the booster equipment. *Jane Lilley*

Motor. The complete set including the Auxiliary Generator was mounted on a welded steel support frame. The frame was riveted to the main underframe longitudinals. The booster set was self-ventilated.

The Booster Generator acted in two different ways, either as a motor or as a generator depending on the control notch selected.

The Booster Motor was also a direct-current machine, and its use was threefold. Firstly, it was used as a motor to drive the Booster Generator up to speed when the booster set was started up. Starting the booster was controlled by the camshaft, whereby a series resistance was cut out in six steps under current limit relay control. Camshaft control replaced the individual contactors that had been used on the Southern Railway Co-Co locomotives. This eliminated the troublesome interlocks which had plagued the earlier locomotives. When the locomotive was started and Notch One was engaged, the Booster Motor was driven by the Booster Generator which was acting at this point as a motor. From Notch Seventeen onwards the Booster Motor worked as a motor, driving the Booster Generator.

To maintain electrical power over gaps in the conductor rail, two large flywheels, with a combined weight of approximately 2,000lb, were fitted to the set's shaft. The kinetic energy produced, maintained a reasonably constant voltage at all times, so preventing surging of the train when in motion. The flywheels had an electro-pneumatic rim brake to stop the set quickly if required.

Control System

Control of the traction motor voltage was either by 'bucking' or 'boosting' the line supply by variation of the booster generator excitation. This was done by an electrically driven camshaft from the driver's controller.

The master controller had two handles. The master switch had four positions, 'off', 'forward', 'neutral' and 'reverse'. The main controller had five positions, 'off', run back', 'hold', 'notch up', and 'run up'. A more basic controller was provided on the driver's assistant side to assist with shunting movements. This controller had no 'run up' position.

When moving the locomotive, the driver would first start up the booster set. With the booster set running at full speed, the master switch handle would then be moved to either the 'forward' or 'reverse' position, with the master controller handle moved to the 'notch up' position. The control camshaft advances one notch and then stops. By moving the controller handle to 'hold' and then to 'notch up', the camshaft moves up another notch. By repeating this, notching can be continued to the maximum.

The controller had multiple notches. The first fifteen notches saw the Booster Generator used as a motor. At Notch Sixteen, the Back Electro-Magnetic Force (BEMF) of the Traction Motors was sufficient to oppose the line voltage with no assistance from the Booster Generator, whose field at this notch was switched off. From Notch Seventeen onwards, the Booster Generator operated as a generator, its input used to boost or assist the line voltage. As the controller was moved upwards through the notches so the generator's voltage increased. A gauge on the driver's desk indicated which of the 33 notches had been selected.

To reduce power, the main controller would be moved back to the 'run back' position. If power were to be shut off completely, the main controller would be moved to the 'off' position' when the camshaft ran back.

The finally agreed style for the cab front. The prominent footstep was used by staff when fixing the 'Golden Arrow' regalia in place, and was a late addition to the design. *Jane Lilley*

Left: **The driver's controls, the brake valves are on the left, with the Master Switch to the right of the brakes. In the foreground are the wheelslip control buttons.** *Simon Lilley.*

Below: **The driver's position in the cab. The cabs were somewhat basic especially when compared to those of the West Coast Mainline AC electric locomotives which arrived a few months later.** *Jane Lilley*

Right: The duplicate controls provided on the assistant's side for use during shunting movements. *Jane Lilley*

Below: The assistant's position was even more basic with just a tip-up seat to sit on. Duplicate controls were provided for use during shunting movements. *Jane Lilley*

The return plug for the ETH supply. These were painted green initially, changing to orange with the advent of BR blue. *Jane Lilley*

Auxiliary equipment

A smaller auxiliary generator was provided, driven by an extension of the Booster Generator. This acted solely as a generator, providing 110 volts for battery charging, the control equipment, battery exhauster, and locomotive lighting.

Batteries

The Nife F8 batteries were located in boxes attached to the underside of the locomotive underframe. These provided 110 volts for lighting, Booster set control, and the auxiliary equipment including the Compressors, Exhausters, and Pantograph.

Livery

Professor Misha Black was also involved in the livery design, in addition to his work on the locomotives' styling. Discussions on a possible livery style began in earnest in the late summer of 1957 when Professor Black wrote to Mr M. G. Burrows of the Southern's CM&EE's department on 2 August. Aside from the main colour to be used, Black said there were other issues to be resolved, in particular the positioning of the lining and the location of the BR crests.

The choice of which shade of green to use, was debated over many months in a number of letters and memoranda between the Southern Region's management, their counterparts at the BTC, and Professor Black. On 23 August 1957 David McKenna the Southern Region's Assistant General Manager wrote to George Williams on the subject. Mr McKenna expressed the view that with coaching stock due to be repainted in what was known as 'Approved shade No 11', having locomotives in the same colour would look better. George Williams was interested in an alternative shade suggesting '2.5 BG 3/6' from the Munsell range instead. Keen to get an idea of how this would look in use, on 29 August 1957 he asked Misha Black for the dimensions of the red and white lining he was proposing so that a panel could be made up using this shade of green with the red and white lining then under consideration. The wish though to use a non-standard shade of green, albeit one used for coaching stock, required Design Panel approval. In the meantime standard BR green should be considered the colour to be used.

Ronald Jarvis, in charge of the design work at Brighton, was also pressing for a decision on the main body colour as Professor Black relayed to George Williams on 24 October. Black added that there were a number of other issues to be

Middle: **The ETH jumper cable was originally located on the cab front, but was soon moved to this location by the driver's side buffer. Later locomotives had the ETH jumper cable mounted here from new.** *Simon Lilley*

Left: **The locomotives' first livery was SR carriage green, lined with a red line edged with two thinner white lines.** *Simon Lilley*

The first of the class, No E5000, at Durnsford Road after delivery from Doncaster. The position of the BR totem and numbers would be altered for later examples, and only this locomotive had the red painted axlebox covers. *British Railways*

resolved. The cab interior colour scheme was one, another was the bodyside lining colour. He suggested using the grey then starting to be used on the new diesels of various types being built or else a white/red/white combination. It had been suggested that the first locomotive, which would be ready in the middle of 1958, should be tested whilst still in grey undercoat, with the second locomotive painted, lined, and completed in every detail first.

The following month saw a flurry of correspondence within the BTC itself on the main question of the livery colour to be used. This started on 4 November with Christian Barman asking the BTC's CME Roland Bond what colour to be used as the Southern Region's CM&EE had been making enquiries. Barman's perhaps obvious suggestion was Southern Region green. In parallel, the following day George Williams wrote to Misha Black telling him that the livery discussion was on hold but that the Southern Region wanted carriage green used. This view was reinforced by Roland Bond's reply to Barman on 5 November. He queried why instructions were needed, as the first locomotive was not due to be completed until late 1958 and also that he was not prepared to go against existing BTC instructions on locomotive liveries. In the light of Bond's letter, George Williams wrote to Misha Black saying the matter was in abeyance for now as the proposed green colour was one not approved by the Commission.

The cab interior colour scheme was also causing some debate, and again there were various exchanges of correspondence between Misha Black, Ronald Jarvis and H. H. Swift in the period between November 1957 and May 1958. On 29 November 1957, Black wrote to Jarvis with his proposals for the cab interior and the materials to be used. He also made arrangements for samples of his preferred materials to be prepared in the various colours for inspection by both BTC and Southern Region officials.

Mr Jarvis replied to Black on the matter on 31 March 1958. He said that the Eastern Region CME K. J. Cook had reported that some of the proposed materials for the cab interior were non-standard items, most notably the seat moquette, and that changes were being made to the floor lino. The letter also advised Black that the train heating socket was being moved to a position underneath the right-hand buffer and that a foot step was being added to the cab front. Professor Black replied two days later, agreeing to these changes. He added that he was pleased that construction was proceeding and was looking forward to seeing the first completed locomotive in around two months' time.

After much discussion, the Design Panel meeting held on 3 June 1958 acceded to the Southern Region's request that their new electric locomotives could be painted in the lighter Southern Region carriage green and not the darker Brunswick Green being used on the new diesel locomotives. It seems though that the discussion did not end at that point. On 10 September, Design Panel member Mr J. Bloomfield wrote to George Williams. In his letter he said that the Design Research Unit were saying that the livery would be decided when the first locomotive was completed, which should be in about six weeks' time. They had also been told that the shade of green to be used would be decided when a sample of Southern Region carriage green was available.

The debate continued on into October when Bloomfield wrote to Christian Barman. Bloomfield said that the BTC's Assistant CME E. S. Cox was also not in favour of SR green for the new locomotives. Cox's view was that he would rather not have the first locomotive in a colour scheme that may not be applied to all of the class given the publicity the first example would attract. It would be better to use either the second or third locomotive as a guinea-pig instead. As for the lining, he thought that had already been agreed and did not want the

Above: **By the time the fifth locomotive No E5004 was complete some changes had been made to the livery. The locomotive number was now level with the red and white lining band and the BR totem was now placed centrally below waist level on both sides.** *British Railways*

Right: **HA Electric Locomotive Main Equipment Layout**

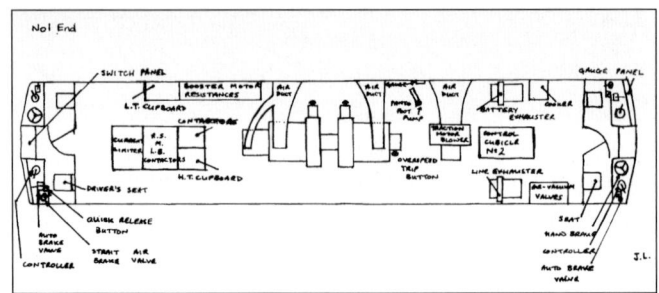

Design Research Unit working on another scheme. Bloomfield ended by saying that he felt Cox might want to consider another colour other than green altogether!

In the midst of all this, the first locomotive was nearing completion. As a result on 12 December BTC CME J. F. Harrison wrote to Barman regarding the livery to be used. No instructions he said, had been given to Doncaster so as the Design Panel had agreed to use Southern Region green he had instructed Doncaster to use that colour. George Williams replied to Harrison four days later, confirming this as the shade of green to be used. The question of lining though was to be discussed at Doncaster on 18 December when he and Misha Black would be there to inspect the first locomotive. Williams added that the Design Panel would like to reconsider the livery for these locomotives and may wish to make alternative suggestions. George Williams also wrote to Misha Black that day. He said that Southern Region green was to be used and that the region's General Manager C. P. Hopkins wanted the same lining as had been applied to the three Co-Co electric locomotives. Mr Williams said he was unsure about using green and would like to discuss finding an alternative in the coming year.

The first locomotive No E5000 was inspected at Doncaster on 18 December 1958 by R. G. Jarvis and Misha Black. Black wrote to Jarvis four days later congratulating him on what he described as a 'really excellent locomotive'. There were some details though that he was less happy with. The central cover straps he felt marred the locomotive's 'massive form', and he was also concerned about the less than perfect finish to the removable louvres. This had resulted in bad joints between the louvres and the bodyside.

Black also wrote to George Williams the same day on the visit to Doncaster. The final issues with lining and the position of the crests were decided according to the letter 'with the painters waiting to finish the locomotive ready for the press launch on 29 December'. In this letter Professor Black made a number of suggestions regarding slight changes to some design details including the use of chromium plate numbers instead of the standard transfers, and a re-positioning of the BR crests.

The eventual livery used was similar to that which had been adopted in 1956 for the three former Southern Railway Co-Co locomotives. The bodysides SR were carriage green and at waist height a 2¾in-wide, white/red/white lining band was applied between the cabs. The bufferbeam between the buffers was red, the bogies black, and the roof grey. The BR totem was placed centrally on both sides below the lining band, although when first built Nos E5000 and E5001 had theirs placed higher on the air intake side between two intakes at the number one end. Both were later altered in line with the rest of the class. The cabside number position also varied at first. The first two locomotives had their numbers above the level of the lining band when built, whereas from No E5002 onwards the numbers were positioned level with the lining band; No E5001 was later altered to conform.

Route Availability

The HA locomotives were classified as 'Route Availability 6'. This meant there were very few electrified lines that were barred to them. The exceptions being the centre lines and the Up and Down slow lines across Charing Cross Bridge which were prohibited. They were also forbidden to use the through lines between Blackfriars Hill Street Junction and Loughborough Junction and the Thames River Bridge No 29 between Gunnersbury and Kew Gardens although in the latter case these could be used in an emergency. A speed restriction of 10mph was also imposed were they to cross the St Paul's River Bridge No10 on the Up and Down loop lines.

3
Testing and Commissioning

Above: **The two 'booster' types together. No E5002 is stabled next to No 20003 at Stewarts Lane depot soon after the Class HA locomotive was delivered.** *Class 47 Preservation Project Archive*

As the newly built locomotives reached the Southern Region, so they were used on a variety of test trains. This was to ensure that each locomotive could be accepted into traffic and also to determine the new type's capabilities. The pioneer locomotive, No E5000, arrived at Durnsford Road Wimbledon on 3 January 1959. After a series of tests there, it ran light engine to Brighton.

The first Electrification Committee meeting of 1959 was held on 15 January. Mr Weedon in charge of the driver training programme was promised he would have the first locomotive on 19 January. Weedon himself said that further changes were being made to the training programme as a combination of staff annual leave and increased traffic from March onwards would reduce the availability of footplate staff so hindering the intended driver training programme. He added that he was still short of one of the three Instructors required.

Just under two weeks later, on 26 January, No E5000 arrived at Stewarts Lane. At this stage work was still ongoing to prepare the depot for electric traction which meant it had to be shunted into the new running shed by a steam locomotive as the third-rail that had been laid was not yet been energised.

The new locomotive spent much of its first few weeks on the Southern Region undergoing trials. The week ending 24 January saw it running between Victoria and Newhaven with loads of either 12 or 14 coaches. January 1959 also saw No E5000 scheduled to make a number test runs to Gillingham and Maidstone for driver training. The second locomotive, No E5001, arrived at Stewarts Lane on 4 February and was temporarily placed in store in the new running shed. No E5000 however continued its trials; on 13 February it took 12 coaches

Barely a month old, on 16 July 1959, No E5007 was used on a test train between Victoria and Newhaven. Here the locomotive is seen passing South Croydon. *Class 47 Preservation Project Archive*

from Victoria to Newhaven. It then moved on to Angerstein Wharf on 24 February for further tests to be carried out there. Here several trips were run over the length of the branch using the recently installed overhead wire system. The same day, No E5002 was released from Doncaster and towed south by BR '9F' No 92202.

With locomotives starting to arrive at the rate of one per month, the Southern Region was able to start to implement the practical part of the driver training programme. Staff had been undergoing classroom tuition since November 1958. This training was undertaken at Stewarts Lane, where a new school for instruction on electric traction opened on 19 November 1958. The school was located in a new building behind the motive power depot. Two classrooms were set aside for multiple-unit training, with the third for locomotive tuition.

Drivers from the existing footplate staff were selected to be trained on the new electric locomotives, the classes catering for 12 drivers at a time. All the participants were already passed as steam drivers or firemen. The three-week course started with a general introduction and description of the vehicles on the first day; this was followed on the second day by looking at the basic principles of electricity. The remainder of the week was given over to tuition on the main pieces of equipment including the traction motors, booster sets, auxiliary generators, motor controllers and compressors.

Emphasis was placed on possible sources of failure. The first part of week two covered the brake equipment, whilst the second half of the week covered the main locomotive preparation and disposal duties.

The third week was based on practical instruction, with two running trips each day. The morning working was to Sevenoaks via Swanley, returning via Orpington, while that in the afternoon was to Maidstone East. Three trainees rode in each locomotive cab with the Instructor. Each trainee in the front cab had some time driving the locomotive while those in the rear concentrated on studying the control panel instruments. By the time Phase Two of the Kent Coast scheme was competed, 144 drivers had qualified to drive the new electric locomotives.

Meanwhile, No E5002 was being put through its paces. On 13 March it made two test runs between Victoria and Newhaven. The train comprised of 14 coaches weighing 464 tons. The main aim of the run was to work the locomotive hard in order to check the commutation of the new locomotive. No E5002 was the first of the class to have a booster with conventional lap windings as compared to the duplex wave windings on the first two locomotives. The duplex wave wound sets were soon found to be suffering commutation problems due to current imbalance between the two windings. Amongst those on board the train that day was Dennis Lightband, from English Electric Co Ltd. The tests proved satisfactory and lap windings became the norm from thereon.

On 15 and 22 March, No E5000 was used on freight trials between Norwood, Redhill, and Three Bridges. Although the locomotive's haulage capacity proved most satisfactory, concerns were raised about its braking capability with unfitted trains. No E5000 was a busy locomotive for on 23 March it was used on a series of 11-coach test trains to Gillingham on timings of 55, 56, and 58 minutes.

A brand new no E5009 outside Doncaster works on 8 August 1959 waiting to be towed down to Stewarts Lane. The shoegear has been fitted although it will be removed for the journey south.
Class 47 Preservation Project Archive

With all three of the Central Division's Co-Co electric locomotives unavailable, on 6 April one of the new HA locomotives was used instead on a regular electric locomotive duty between New Cross Gate, Norwood, and Lewes.

A week later No E5003 was delivered, meaning that by April, four of the 13 locomotives had arrived. On 10 April, at the Electrification Committee it was said that it was important that locomotives were made available well before the 15 June commencement date for Phase One. This would help to alleviate the problems caused by the delivery delays and enable the benefits to be reaped of practical traffic experience. Mr Sykes promised that locomotives would indeed be handed over at the earliest possible date after delivery. As if to prove the point just a few weeks after entering service, No E5003 was commandeered by the Central Division and was noted being used on an engineer's train at Brighton station.

All however was not plain sailing. All of the five locomotives delivered to date had to be taken out of service between 22 April and 11 May. A circuit breaker fitted to No E5002 had failed. As a result, new circuit breakers had to be made, fitted, and tested before the locomotives could re-enter service.

One locomotive was indeed made available for crew training on 11 May. At the Electrification Committee meeting on 14 May, Mr Smyth said that efforts were being made to release further locomotives for crew training without delay. Mr Weedon reiterated the need for as many locomotives as possible to be available prior to the start date of 15 June for electric services.

By the time of the next meeting on 11 June, there was more progress to report. Seven out of the 13 locomotives had now been delivered. Three locomotives were now in traffic and seven were promised to be available for use when electric services started four days later.

The Phase Two Locomotives

Before even the first locomotive had been delivered for Phase One, plans were well advanced for the ordering of an additional 11 locomotives that were required for Phase Two. Originally, it had been planned to include them in their submission for the 1961 Building Programme, so long as the programme was authorised in September 1959. However, in a letter to R. C. Bond, now the Technical Advisor to the BTC, the Southern Region said they wished for the 11 locomotives to be included in the 1960 programme as this would ensure both continuity of production at Doncaster and enable locomotives to be available in good time for driver training.

The 11 were authorised by the BTC on 20 November 1958 at a cost £671,000 (£61,000 each). It was estimated the scrap value of the steam locomotives displaced by their construction was £11,570, giving a net outlay of £659,430. The order for their electrical equipment was authorised by the Supply Committee on 6 March 1959 at a cost of £410,300. As this was both an extension to an existing order already approved by the BTC and came under the terms of the Southern Region/English Electric 10-year agreement, no further authorisation was required.

In a number of locations such as Faversham as we see here a basic overhead wire system was installed. This was felt to be much safer for yard staff than a third rail. *Class 47 Preservation Project Archive*

The Rail Joint Tests 1959

In May 1959, a series of rail joint tests between Three Bridges and Balcombe Tunnel Junction were carried out. The aim of the tests was to evaluate the rail end stresses under the E5000 Bo-Bo electric locomotives, and their comparison with the effects created by other locomotive types including the Southern Region's Co-Co locomotives Nos 20001 and 20002, BRCW Type 2s Nos D5309 and D5312, the latter having been borrowed from the Eastern Region. The two HA type locomotives used in these tests were Nos E5003 and E5004.

There were eight test sections about 10 chains in length on the up through line, between 30 miles 49 chains and 31 miles and 50 chains. There was one test section on the down through line between 31 miles 7 chains and 31 miles 27 chains. The up line sections had been laid in August 1958 and the down line section back in May 1956 as part of planned track renewals. On 25 May Nos 20001 and 20002 made 10 passes over the area at speeds between 2mph to 40mph, whilst various service trains comprising of mainly COR/BUF and 5BEL stock passed over the various joints at 75mph. The following day the two locomotives made a further 10 test runs at speeds which varied between 45mph and 80mph. Some Victoria to Brighton services consisting of various types of EMU stock were also tested at 60mph. The pair of Type 2s carried out 12 runs on 27 May at speeds between 2 and 75mph. The following day the various passenger trains passed over the test area at 20mph whilst a special train comprising of two 4CEP units and the Motor Luggage Van (MLV) No S68001 made five runs at various speeds from 20 to 90mph. The final day of testing was 29 May, which saw Nos E5003 and E5004 tested at speeds ranging between 2 and 108mph.

Early Work and Phase Two

The Phase One engineering work was completed at the end of May 1959, and electric running began shortly afterwards. The honour of hauling the first electric service between London and Ramsgate fell to No E5004 on 2 June when it was used on the 8:00am from Victoria and return. There was a second electric departure from Victoria at 3:10pm using No E5003. No E5004 was used again that day hauling the 8:00pm to Dover and return.

Their first prestige passenger work was on the heavily loaded 'Night Ferry', first working the train on 8 June, a week before Phase One started full operation. The train consisted of No E5003 hauling five corridors, seven sleeping cars, and two luggage vans weighing around 610 tons gross. Although the 'Night Ferry' had been turned over to electric traction, steam had a last hurrah that weekend. On the Friday evening the train was worked by 'L1' No 31753 and 'Battle of Britain' No 34068 *Kenley*. The Saturday night train was hauled by 'Merchant Navy' No 35015 *Rotterdam Lloyd*.

No E5003 was used each day until the morning of 12 June when all the HA locomotives then in service were stopped to change brake blocks. A block had broken on No E5001 at Meopham when on a driver training trip. One half of the block fell from the locomotive whilst travelling at speed, causing damage to some of the leading carriages. On closer examination it was found that the block holders had been made incorrectly and the safety straps were missing. After a short interlude, electric working of the 'Night Ferry' resumed on 14 June with No E5003 provided for that night's departure from Victoria.

The first 'electric' timetable started on 15 June and with a number of freight duties also now allocated to the class. Their introduction was gradual as only six locomotives had been delivered and not all of these had yet been accepted into traffic. In that first timetable there were just 10 weekday services booked for electric locomotives, with five on a Sunday. Another Sunday only service was scheduled to start on 17 September when more locomotives would be available. From 20 September a conditional service was added to their duties. If required, it ran from Southwark to Dover Marine, leaving at 3.48am and arriving at 7am.

In addition to these initial freight duties, the class were allocated some passenger, parcels, and newspaper trains. Some of these would become regular duties for them for many years to come.

The up 'Night Ferry' service had a relief train available if required. This was booked to leave Dover Marine at 8.5am arriving at Victoria at 9.38am. A regular parcels duty for them was the 5.3am Faversham to Dover Priory parcels which also carried newspapers and passenger. On Sundays they were used on the 4.20am newspaper train from Victoria to Dover Priory and the 7.18am Faversham to Dover Marine passenger, parcels, and fish train.

July also saw them used on some boat train services between Victoria and Newhaven on the Central Division. The class were also running test trains on the division at the time, both Nos E5001 and E5007 used in the middle of the month. The locomotives were also starting to be used on other duties, one example of this was when on Sunday 23 August No E5003 took over a Bedford to Margate excursion at Clapham Junction.

Meanwhile the Electrification Committee continued with their monthly meetings as work on Phase Two progressed. The locomotives for Phase One had been delivered late, and committee members were given something of a bombshell regarding the 11 Phase Two locomotives when they met on 17 September. Mr Sykes told them that the Eastern Region had omitted to place an order for the locomotives' exhausters until August. The lead time for this essential equipment was between eight and nine months, meaning they would not be delivered to Doncaster until May 1960 at the earliest. If the locomotives were delivered without their exhausters fitted they could only be used on unfitted freight services, or somewhat pointless light engine movements. Mr Fitch had been asked for his views on whether the locomotives should be accepted or stored until the exhausters could be fitted.

On 29 September Mr Fitch recommended that acceptance of the affected locomotives be

An almost brand new No E5017 stands at Faversham awaiting its next duty during the summer of 1960. This was one of the Phase Two locomotives delivered without exhausters which had to be fitted at Eastleigh before the locomotives could enter service.
Class 47 Preservation Project Archive

deferred until they were fully equipped. His reasoning was that the locomotives would be used on Phase One work and all would be under-employed until work on Phase Two had been completed. Mr Weedon, in charge of the driver training scheme, said that deferring delivery would cause the Eastern Region problems, and that he was willing to have one or two locomotives without exhausters to use for training purposes.

In the meantime, those locomotives built under Phase One were being put to work. The 'Night Ferry' had a difficult journey on 18 October when a brake defect meant a late departure from Victoria, with a subsequent stop at Bromley South to remove the coach with defective brakes. Nine days later the up 'Night Ferry', already running late, was further delayed when the HA locomotive in charge failed at Sole Street. The last of the first batch was delivered on 27 October.

On several occasions during the autumn of 1959, No E5000 was noted running without its pantograph. The first was in September when seen at Ramsgate and then again on 2 November when at Faversham. This was not uncommon and locomotives running in such a condition would usually be restricted to the main passenger diagram covering the 'Golden Arrow' and 'Night Ferry' services.

An early technical problem for the class was traction motor armature failure due to over-speeding. Two locomotives were affected in consecutive days in October. Firstly on 26 October at Lee Junction, and then the following day with the train locomotive on the down 'Night Ferry'. On both occasions the locomotives were travelling at between 30 and 50mph when the wheels slipped. If the wheelspin was left uncontrolled, the safe armature speed limit could be exceeded so causing excessive stress on the armature with the result that it 'burst'.

Further investigations into the problem were carried out with a series of test trains run on Wednesday 25 and Thursday 26 November from Victoria to Dover. The train with No E5009 at the head, was made up of the London Midland Region's dynamometer car No 3, coincidentally the same vehicle as had been used for tests with Co-Co booster locomotive No 20003 back in 1951, a bogie brake followed by 10 hopper wagons, with another bogie brake van at the rear made up the load. This gave a total weight of some 700 tons, and was close to that of the 'Night Ferry' train. The trains left Victoria at 10:43am and travelled to Dover via Chatham, stopping each way at Canterbury East. The return journeys terminated at Stewarts Lane, having left Dover Marine at 2.10pm. The tests were due to run for three days, but were cancelled on Friday 27 November. Instead dynamometer car No 3 was quickly returned to the LMR being taken from Stewarts Lane to St Pancras. As a result of these tests, a simple wheelspin protection system was then developed and fitted to the class. This is described in greater detail in Chapter 6.

November 1959 was not a good month for the class. Early in the month it was reported that nine of the class were out of use at the same time. One member had failed at Northfleet on 3 November, and another at Plumstead four days later. However it was not all doom and gloom. A member of the class hauling ordinary coaches was used in place of the usual two two-car EMU on the 8:18am Faversham to Dover service calling at all stations. The London bound 'Night Ferry' was noted passing Canterbury East behind No E5009 some 90 minutes late on 14 November, though no reason was given. In fairness however, the inbound 'Night Ferry' service was always liable to run late if the ferry from Dunkirk was late.

By November the ramifications of the late ordering of the exhausters for the second batch were becoming much clearer. The first three locomotives would be delivered complete. Two of the three would be delivered in December 1959, with the third in January 1960. The next six though would be delivered incomplete. Mr Sykes told the Electrification Committee on 12 November that the locomotives would have to be stored, preferably somewhere on the region, until the missing equipment arrived and was fitted. The minutes have been annotated by an unknown hand 'Isn't any kind of running better than storage?'

The first of the second batch, No E5013, arrived on 9 December, complete. A suitable storage site for the incomplete locomotives had still to be found. Although all of the first 13 locomotives had been delivered and accepted into traffic, there were still occasions early in their service lives when members of the class were unavailable for their booked work such as on 11 December when one of their parcels duties, routed via the North Kent Line, had to be worked by rebuilt 'West Country' No 34027 *Taw Valley*.

4
The 1960s

Above: **During the BTC's Electrification Conference held in October 1960, an exhibition was arranged of electric locomotives and multiple-units at Battersea Wharf. The brand new No E5022 was chosen to represent the HA type.** *Class 47 Preservation Project Archive*

Whilst the Southern Region had been expecting three locomotives from the second batch to have been delivered by January 1960 it was only one that had arrived by the time of the Electrification Committee's first meeting of the year on 14 January. In addition the search for a suitable storage location for the locomotives that would be delivered incomplete (without the exhausters) continued.

Operationally the route taken by the 'Night Ferry' did not vary on the Southern Region. Unusual perhaps but necessary due to operational timings, the international nature of the train and related customs restrictions, so it was a surprise when on 31 January and due to engineering works at Victoria the train was diverted via Crystal Palace.

Construction continued at Doncaster and Nos E5014 and E5015 left there on 23 February, both without exhausters. Although the region was continuing to look for a suitable storage site for these incomplete locomotives, no problems had been experienced in accommodating them so far. The next locomotive delivered was No E5017 on 24 March. The examples without exhausters were all taken to Eastleigh works to await the arrival of the missing equipment. The Eastleigh works records show that No E5014 arrived there on 2 March, with just seven miles 'on the clock'. (A slightly strange calculation as the distance from Doncaster to Eastleigh was in the hundreds but the figure quoted related to 'miles under own power'.) No E5015 arrived just over three weeks later without any mileage attributed to it. The late running No E5016 left Doncaster on 5 April, and took exactly three weeks to arrive at Eastleigh. During that time it had obviously seen some use as it had 73 miles recorded against it when it entered the works.

O. S. Nock's 'British Locomotive Practice and Performance' column within the *Railway Magazine* for April 1960 provided an early indication of the new locomotives' capabilities and haulage capacity. In his column, Nock provided details of a test train run between London and Dover. With the train weighing 695 tons, the unidentified locomotive, climbed the 1 in 132 gradient between Adisham and Snowdown at a sustained speed of 60mph. The drawbar horsepower recorded was 2,700 dbhp. At speeds below 65mph Nock observed that the drawbar horsepower was greater than that of the English Electric Type 5 diesels ('Deltics').

The time these incomplete locomotives spent at Eastleigh awaiting completion varied widely. No E5017 was finished and released into traffic on 14 May. In comparison, No E5018 which had arrived at Eastleigh on 9 May did not leave until 3 December. Whilst at Eastleigh, the locomotives were examined closely and the opportunity taken to rectify any faults found.

The 1960 summer timetable began on 13 June and showed the number of freight duties turned over to electric traction was a significant increase, indeed around double the number of turns compared to the previous timetable. The number of locomotives available was also significantly larger than during much of the previous timetable. There were now 21 trains allocated to the class that ran every day, with a further 20 Monday to Saturday services. Seven Sunday-only services were also now allocated to electric traction, along with a number of other services running on specified days only. Locations such as Dover, Hither Green, and Hoo Junction saw significant numbers of electrically hauled freight services during any given 24 hours. The newly installed overhead wiring at some locations also saw use at locations such as Snowdown Colliery and Angerstein Wharf, with several trains arriving and leaving these locations every day.

This timetable saw the class increase the number of passenger and parcels duties they had. Of these the most notable passenger duty was the 'Night Ferry'. The London bound service left Dover at 7.20am each morning arriving at Victoria at 9.10am. There was also a provision for a relief train for the 'Night Ferry' in this timetable. Electric locomotive hauled also, this left Dover at 8.05am arriving at Victoria at 9.46, albeit a slower journey than with the previous timetable. The outbound service left Victoria at 10pm in the summer months arriving at Dover at 11.42pm. In the winter months, between 3 October 1960 and 14 April 1961, the departure was earlier at 9pm with an arrival time at Dover of 10.42pm. All these timings applied throughout the week from Monday to Sunday.

Several parcels services were also electrically hauled, bringing the locomotives into Cannon Street and Holborn Viaduct stations, for example the 3am from Holborn Viaduct to Ramsgate which carried passengers as well as newspapers and parcels. With a number of stops en route to off load people, newspapers, and parcels, Ramsgate was not reached until 5.58am. The overall pattern of work was similar on a Sunday, but with a reduced number of workings.

In addition to their allocated work on the South Eastern Division there was now a freight diagram for them on the Central Division which started on 17 September. This was a Saturday night turn where the locomotive in question left Stewarts Lane at 7.25pm and first running light engine to Bricklayers Arms, arriving there at 8.14pm. Here it would take the 8:42pm freight to Horsham, with a scheduled arrival at 11.01pm. It would leave there at 3.00am on the Sunday morning heading back into London to Norwood Yard. Upon arrival there at 5.42, it left soon after, to run light back to Stewarts Lane with a scheduled arrival time of 6.20am.

The 'Golden Arrow' headboard as used in the 'electric' era along with one of the bodyside golden arrows, now happily on display in the NRM at York. The background of the arrow's flights has been painted BR blue to match the locomotive bodyside colour. *Simon Lilley*

An unidentified member of the class with a coal train from the Kent coalfield. *Class 47 Preservation Project Archive*

A proud passenger poses next to No E5006 at Victoria prior to departure with the 'Golden Arrow'. The locomotive is carrying the full train regalia of headboard, flags, and bodyside arrow. The 13 headcode indicates a service to Dover Marine via Catford and Maidstone East, rather than the usual route through Herne Hill and Orpington. Interestingly, whilst the locomotive is in unlined green, it has yet to be fitted with cab rain strips.
Class 47 Preservation Project Archive

Above: Either No E5005 has just been used on the 'Night Ferry', or is about to be in this view taken at Stewarts Lane. Whilst No E5005 is in unlined green and has received cab rain strips, the other Class HA in the picture retains its original livery and has yet to be fitted with rain strips. The grilles on the 'A' side of No E5005 have been removed and plated over leaving just the centre droplight window in place. The headboard is the second type of 'Night Ferry' board used during the electric era.
Class 47 Preservation Project Archive

Left: Over several years a series of rail joint tests were carried out between Three Bridges, Haywards Heath and Balcombe. No E5004 is seen leading SR Co-Co No 20001 and BRCW Type 3 No D6506 near Balcombe on Sunday 17 July 1960. No E5004 has been fitted with headcode blinds with the smaller characters but the ETH jumper cable is in its original position still on the cab front. *Class 47 Preservation Project Archive*

On 7 July Co-Co electric locomotive No 20001 failed when working the 5.14pm Newhaven to Victoria boat train. With No 20001 then stopped for repairs, HA No E5017 was borrowed from the South Eastern Division to cover No 20002's freight duties so that it in turn could be used on the Newhaven boat trains.

A week later, the Electrification Committee met. Six locomotives had now been delivered without exhausters, the latest being No E5020 on 16 June, though this would prove to be the last example delivered in such a condition.

With the work for Phase Two well underway, one of the side issues relating to the scheme was resolved. With electrification, the 'Golden Arrow' Pullman service would be electrically hauled. Discussions with the Pullman Car Co Ltd as to who would pay for the fitting of the 17 cars used on the service reached agreement when on 24 June the Southern Region General Manager Mr C. P. Hopkins agreed to recommend to the Southern Area Board that they pay the £20,400 estimated cost of the work. This would be charged to the overall costs of the Phase Two scheme. Initial thoughts on this issue had also included removing Pullman cars from the 6PUL units and converting them into multiple-units for use on the 'Golden Arrow' service.

Ten days later, on Sunday 17 July, the now repaired Co-Co electric locomotive No 20001 along with HA electric locomotive No E5004 and BRCW Type 3 No D6506 was used for a further series of rail joint tests on the Brighton mainline between Three Bridges and either Balcombe or Haywards Heath. These tests were carried out in both directions with the leading locomotive hauling the other two.

The next locomotive, No E5021, was delivered on 27 July. Whilst it was at least exhauster fitted, it was instead missing other parts and so was held out of traffic with those locomotives still awaiting exhausters until the relevant parts arrived and could be fitted.

The middle of August saw No E5005 used on the Newhaven boat trains as the Co-Co electric locomotives Nos 20002 and 20003 were out of service. The HA locomotives could only be used on the Newhaven services in the summer months as the stock used was steam-heat only. This meant that in the winter months if one of the Co-Co electric locomotives was unavailable steam traction had to deputise.

With around 18 months of service under their belts, their capabilities were assessed for the first time on a service train in the *Railway Magazine* series 'Locomotive Practice and Performance' for August 1960. O. S. Nock described a footplate journey on No E5002 working the 'Night Ferry' from Dover to London. The train weighed 620 tons and the journey was completed in 114 minutes against a booked time of 110 minutes, the four-minute difference due to a permanent way slack and several signal checks. The permanent way slack was near Canterbury, which brought the train's speed down from 68mph to 30mph. Later, having climbed Sole Street bank at a maximum speed of 43mph with the controller on Notch 30, there was a signal check meaning a slowing to 30mph. Nock calculated that No E5002's drawbar horsepower as having reached 2165dbhp before speed had to be reduced.

On the approaches to London there were several more severe signal checks. The first was when passing through Shortlands station. The train then had to negotiate a tricky re-start, up the sharp rise to the junction where there was a considerable 'gap' when crossing over to the Catford Loop line. Further on the train was brought to a complete stand at Cambria Junction and Grosvenor Bridge just outside Victoria was crossed at what was described as a walking pace.

Nock made comparisons with a similar journey made with 'N15' No 30761 *Sir Balan* with a train weighing 425 tons. The 'King Arthur' managed the journey in 143 minutes, against a schedule of 120 minutes. Its progress had been hampered, as with No E5002, by several signal checks, one of which brought the train to a stand at Canterbury.

Throughout their lives, the Class HAs were overhauled at Eastleigh. Until the Bournemouth electrification scheme, they were towed there, in the early days often by steam locomotives, and not always by the most direct route. For example, when No E5010 arrived at Eastleigh on 14 August 1960 for attention it was behind BR Standard 5 No 73118. Ten days later, 'C' class 0-6-0 No 31753 took No E5002 to Eastleigh, returning with No E5006.

There was then a five-week gap until the next locomotive, No E5022, arrived on 1 September. Like No E5021 it was missing some parts and so could not be put into traffic straightaway.

A further series of rail-joint tests were carried out in October 1960. These were Phase 6 of the ongoing research work based around Three Bridges, which tests had several aims. The first concerned running heavily loaded freight wagons at higher speeds. The tests would help determine what effects, if any, the higher speeds had on rail joints. Both the Chief Civil Engineer (CCE) and the CM&EE were also keen to know the effects on rail joints of the new EP multiple-unit stock when running at 90mph. The final aim was a slightly unusual one. It was to ascertain if there was a difference in the effect on rail joints of the two different types of bogie on the London Midland Region's Metropolitan-Vickers Type 2 Co-Bo locomotives.

The freight vehicle tests used vehicles with axle-loads initially up to 22½ tons with a second set of tests using vehicles up to 33½ tons. The tests using 22½-ton wagons were with No E5003 hauling four loaded wagons, three empty ones, two Bulleid coaches and two 20-ton brake vans. These tests produced a set of results which led to the test with nine 33½-ton loaded vehicles.

Right: **One of the main freight duties for the Class 71s in the late 1960s was the block air-brake trains that ran both ways between Hither Green Continental Depot and Dover Marine. No E5011 is seen on one of these trains at Chislehurst Junction. With a headcode of 9D the train would be routed via Chatham.** R. W. Easterby

Below: **Flanked by two other HAs at Hither Green on 19 October 1963, No E5003 awaits its next duty. The locomotive is in its original lined green livery as is No E5002 to the left. The other locomotive in the picture, No E5021, has already succumbed to unlined green.**
Class 47 Preservation Project Archive

Two series of tests were undertaken and two locomotives were used together, Nos E5016 and E5000. This was highly unusual as double heading of these locomotives was certainly not the norm. The make up for the two tests varied, and two wagons had to be removed during the second series of tests as they had become defective. The last run of the second set of tests saw three more wagons removed. The speed range for all the tests started at 5mph and was increased incrementally to around 75mph.

The test results showed that the 33½-ton wagons running at 45mph were in normal circumstances unlikely to cause fatigue damage around the fish plate bolt holes. It was also determined that there was no significant difference in the stresses created by the two different types of bogie on the Co-Bo locomotive running in either direction. The stresses created by the EP multiple-unit stock running at 90 mph were not significantly different to those created by the existing EMU stock on the Brighton line running at 60-70mph. The speed stresses created by the Metropolitan-Vickers Type 2 Co-Bo diesel and the HA Bo-Bo electric locomotives were basically the same. (The test report does not identify which member of the Metropolitan-Vickers Type 2 Co-Bo diesel – Class 28 – was involved.)

In October 1960 the British Railways Electrification Conference was held in London. As part of the proceedings an exhibition of locomotives and equipment was held at Battersea Wharf from 3 to 9 October. Representing the Southern Region, on what was after all home turf, was No E5022 that had been delivered from Doncaster just a month previously.

The day after the conference finished, the new depot for fruit and vegetable traffic from Europe was opened at Hither Green as part of the Phase Two scheme. This replaced the previous facility at Southwark. It was a separate facility from the main yard.

The main shed was over 1,000 feet long and could accommodate 25 ferry vehicles. The trains usually consisted of 24 such wagons usually fully fitted with vacuum brakes. There were four departures a day from Dover at 3.15 am, 10.15 am, 4.35 pm, and 8.49 pm. The 3.15 am train also conveyed vehicles for onward movement to Bricklayers Arms and the 4.35 pm train ran if traffic demands required it.

There were three corresponding daily down trains of empty wagons, this time leaving Hither Green at 4.25 am, 2.10 pm, and 8.26 pm. In the off-peak season the vans were often stored at Faversham given the space constraints at Dover. The 68½-mile journey from Dover to Hither Green via Folkestone, Ashford, Tonbridge and Orpington was scheduled to take 84½ minutes. On arrival at Hither Green the locomotive would switch from third rail to overhead wire current collection, overhead wires having been installed on the six reception roads so the HA locomotive could continue to take power. The wagons would then be moved into the main shed by a diesel shunter.

The HA locomotives were never named. However, there is some evidence to indicate this might have been a possibility. The Brighton Drawing Office produced a drawing on 26 October entitled 'New Position for Nameplate'. There is no other reference in the drawing register to indicate as to where nameplates might have been located, but this drawing would seem to indicate it was something that was considered at one point. No suggested names are mentioned.

When the Electrification Committee met on 10 November, they heard that No E5023 had been delivered on 25 October. Like the two previous examples it had been built with a vacuum exhauster, but various other parts were missing and so it was stored until those parts were available and could be fitted.

No E5003 was taken part way to Eastleigh by Class 'H' No 31317 on 8 January 1961. The route taken from Stewarts Lane to Chichester was via Dorking. There, an Eastleigh based locomotive took No E5003 back with it, having brought the ex-works No E5002 with it. No E5002 was taken to Stewarts Lane later in the day behind No 31317.

At the end of January 1961, the Prime Minister Harold Macmillan used the 'Night Ferry' to travel to Rambouillet for talks with the French President General Charles de Gaulle, unfortunately thick fog at Dunkirk meant that Mr Macmillan

No E5014 is seen here on display as part of the exhibition staged by British Railways at Marylebone between 11 and 14 May 1961 which celebrated 50 years of the Institution of Locomotive Engineers.
Class 47 Preservation Project Archive

was half an hour late for his meeting with the President. This also proved to be the last occasion that the 'Night Ferry' was used by a Prime Minister on an official visit, though other ministers continued to use the train until its withdrawal.

The other prestige train allocated to the HAs was the 'Golden Arrow'. This became a booked duty for them following the completion of the electrification scheme to Folkestone and Dover. The first electrically hauled 'Golden Arrow' was 12 June 1961 using an immaculate No E5015 hauling two CCTs, eight Pullman Cars and two ordinary coaches. The locomotive's paint work had been touched up and re-varnished for the occasion. Unfortunately, the train left Dover Marine four minutes late and was further delayed into London by five permanent way slacks, and two signal stops meaning a 13-minute late arrival at Victoria. The summer timetable started on 18 June and now with the 'Golden Arrow' service accelerated. The previous year the steam hauled service had seen both the up and down journeys timed at 107 minutes. Now with electric traction the 'Down' (to Dover) service was cut to 98 minutes, and the 'Up' service to 93 minutes. The 'Night Ferry' journey times remained unaltered. The 'summer' departure time of 10pm ended in November and resumed again at the end of March 1962. The 'winter' departure time stayed at 9.0pm.

The same timetable saw another increase in freight work for the class now that all were in service and both main routes to the Kent coast were now electrified. Steam traction had all but been eliminated and so the main freight flows for the HA locomotives were as before but now more numerous with far greater activity around locations such as Hither Green, Hoo Junction, Snowdown Colliery, and Dover Marine and Dover Town.

For this timetable, there were other passenger trains allocated to the class, in addition to their main passenger duties of the 'Golden Arrow' and 'Night Ferry' services and it was in effect the electrically-worked 'steam railway' timetable of the 12 months preceding the full electric service – electric traction introduced but running to steam timings. The HAs, it was stated officially, also worked a number of passenger services which were unsuitable for EMU operation at the time although no reason is given. These were the 6.18am Cannon Street to Dover (Mon–Fri only), 6.44am Ramsgate to Cannon Street, 7.18am London Bridge to Ramsgate (Mon–Fri only), 4.56pm Cannon Street to Ramsgate (SX), and 10.50pm Charing Cross to Dover (SX). On Saturdays they could be seen on 8.50am Dover to Charing Cross, 11.50am Charing Cross to Deal, and 1.10pm Charing Cross to Ramsgate services. The Charing Cross to Deal service only ran until 9 September. From the following Saturday it terminated at Ashford. The evening rush hour Cannon St to Ramsgate service used a former 'Man of Kent' steam set.

There was also an increase in the number of parcels and newspaper trains now worked by electric traction. Most started or ended in London, but not all. The 3am from Holborn Viaduct carried passengers, parcels, and newspapers and divided at Faversham where one portion went on to Ramsgate and the other to Dover. There were also two other early morning parcels working from London, both leaving at 3.40am.

One of these was from Holborn Viaduct for Ramsgate, the other from Cannon Street also for Ramsgate and which also conveyed fish. There was a further early morning parcels duty from Faversham for Dover Marine leaving at 6.42am.

Whilst the booster equipment was meant to ensure that gaps in the third rail were not an issue, occasionally problems did arise. On 28 June, the locomotive used on the 4.56pm Cannon Street to Ramsgate service became 'gapped' at London Bridge, causing a 20-minute delay to the service. The following month on 28 July, the locomotive used on the 'Night Ferry' service from Victoria that night failed between Bromley South and Bickley. A replacement locomotive was sent from Stewarts Lane with consequent delays.

The class retained their short weekend Central Division freight diagram starting on 23 September, though with some slight changes compared to previously. Departure was earlier from Stewarts Lane at 6.55pm, arriving at Norwood Yard at 7.34pm. From there the locomotive would work the 8.20pm freight to Three Bridges arriving at 9.8pm. After a short break it would then run light engine to Bricklayers Arms in order to haul the 10.37pm freight service to Three Bridges, due to arrive at 12.6am. There would be a two-hour layover there before a light engine journey to Horsham and back – the reason for this latter move and return is not clear. When back again at Three Bridges the locomotive was booked to work the 4.17am freight departure for Norwood Yard. On arriving there, the locomotive would run light back to Stewarts Lane.

British Railways staged an exhibition at Marylebone Goods Yard to celebrate the Golden Jubilee of the Institution of Locomotive Engineers between 11 and 14 May 1961. A number of new locomotives were on display to the public including HA electric locomotive No E5014.

The 'Golden Arrow' throughout its life always had an air of glamour and luxury, being used by the rich and famous to make their way to London. One such occasion was on 7 November 1961 when No E5015 was the locomotive used to bring to London, King Gustav of Sweden, Queen Louise, and their grand-daughter Princess Margaretha on a private visit.

The four-weekly report 'Electric Traction Statistics – Service Performance' gives an indication of the increased utilisation of the HA locomotives once all 24 locomotives were available for traffic. The report included the Southern Region's three Co-Co locomotives in these totals, so the figures cover two different classes and a total of 27 locomotives.

Bad weather on 1 January 1962 meant that steam traction was used on the 'Night Ferry' service to London. Class 'N' No 31412 piloted rebuilt 'West Country' No 34100 *Appledore*. This would prove to be the last recorded instance of steam traction being used for the train. The same day the booked electric locomotive hauling the 'Golden Arrow' from Dover, No E5015, caught fire at Knockholt. A rescue locomotive had to be sent from Hither Green with the result that arrival into London Victoria was two hours late.

On 4 April 1962, Co-Co electric locomotive No 20002 became defective whilst working the 5.14pm Newhaven to Victoria boat train. At Three Bridges HA No E5006 was on hand

Southern Region Electric Locomotive Service Performance 1960 and 1961					
Date	Percentage Available	Train Miles	Locomotive Miles	Traffic Failures	Loco Miles/Failure
31/12/60	63%	49,353	64,523	3	21,505
30/12/61	85.2%	65,230	79,693	3	26,564

to give assistance. This was an unusual combination of the region's two electric locomotive types to say the least. Ten days later, the booked electric locomotive for the 'Golden Arrow' was not available due a failure, this time though there was no return to steam and the train was instead double-headed by BRCW Type 3 No D6536 and a BR/Sulzer Type 2.

Before Phase Two began, a series of tests were conducted to determine the safe way of operating electric trains on the 1 in 30 Folkestone bank. In May, No E5010 was used with a train made up an MLV and two 4CEP units, a combined weight of 337 tons. These tests were conducted on a wet day and the EMUs had to be brought into use to assist No E5010 when it almost slipped to a stand near the top of the bank.

The new fully electric timetable started on 18 June 1962 and the passenger duties the class had during the 1961 timetable were turned over to EMUs. The parcels and newspaper traffic remained basically unchanged. One new passenger duty was the Ramsgate portion of the Monday to Saturday 10.50am Wolverhampton to Margate service. This train divided at Ashford with the Ramsgate portion leaving at 4.21pm. The outward bound train from Ramsgate left at 9.10am, arriving at Ashford at 10.27am. There it joined with the Margate portion which had left there at 9.25am. This service ran until 26 October and resumed on 8 April 1963.

Still included was the short weekend freight diagram on the Central Division, but there were some minor changes compared to the 1961 diagram. The two-hour layover at Three Bridges was changed and a return freight working to Norwood Yard inserted instead. The return light engine journey from Three Bridges to Horsham was kept, before the locomotive left Three Bridges at 4.5am with a working to Norwood Yard. From there the locomotive would run light back to Stewarts Lane with a scheduled arrival time of 5.45am.

With this timetable change, all freight traffic was now either diesel or electrically hauled with many of the heavier trains in the hands of electric locomotives. Some of the coal trains especially from places like Betteshanger could weigh as much as 900 tons.

The timings for the electrically hauled 'Night Ferry' were 98 minutes to Dover, a distance of 78½ miles. The journey to London was timetabled for 110 minutes. This compared to 96 minutes down and 100 minutes up, via Tonbridge for the steam hauled service when introduced in 1936 with a train weighing 400 tons.

This timetable also saw an acceleration of the 'Golden Arrow' journey times. The previous timing of 1 hour 38 minutes from London to Dover became 1 hour 22 minutes. The return journey from Dover was reduced from 1 hour 33 minutes in 1961 to 1 hour 25 minutes.

During November 1962 two of the three Co-Co booster locomotives were out of service. With the HA type also in short supply, the Central Division were unable to borrow any from the South Eastern Division as they had done previously and so steam locomotives had to be used to substitute. By this time the HAs were becoming a feature of the Newhaven boat trains although they were also appearing on other parts of the Central Division.

With the completion of both phases of the Kent Coast scheme the final project costs were calculated during the summer of 1962. It was found that the cost of the 24 electric locomotives had exceeded the authorised amount by some £320,000, some £91,097 of this over-spending on the second batch of 11 locomotives. The reasons for such an overspend fell into four main categories. Firstly there were increases in cost of £157,000 compared to the original estimate and due to the time taken between the locomotives being authorised and them being delivered. Second was the cost of the first batch of 13 locomotives had been under-estimated by a further £75,000, mainly due to increased labour and material costs. Third was increased import duties on equipment from overseas which accounted for a further £34,000 of the over-spend. Finally £53,000 was accounted for by spending on modifications to the locomotives after they had been completed.

On 1 December 1962 No E5000 was renumbered to No E5024, a change that had been intended for some time. A Drivers Instruction Manual from the period advised staff that No E5000 was to be renumbered to No E5024 on its next overhaul. The locomotive entered Eastleigh works for a light casual repair on 30 October 1962 and was released on 1 December to await a tow back to London bearing its new number. Even when the locomotive was renumbered from No E5000 to No E5024 in December 1962, the numbers were still placed in the higher position on the cabside when compared to Nos E5001–E5023. This remained the case until a few years later when the locomotive went to Crewe for rebuilding as an electro-diesel.

In the spring of 1963 No E5023 was seen at Eastbourne on a freight duty on 9 March. This was the first recorded sighting of an HA electric locomotive at the seaside town. *Railway Magazine* was also reporting that both of the region's electric locomotive types, the Co-Cos and the HA Bo-Bos, were working freight trains regularly in the Preston Park area. The trains being marshalled so that they had a 'fitted' head.

The 1963 timetable change happened on 17 June but with the timings of most the class's passenger, parcel, and newspaper services remaining unchanged. The service between Wolverhampton and Margate, of which they worked a portion between Ashford and Ramsgate, was reduced to a Saturdays only service with this timetable. The class were still used on the morning departure from Ramsgate to Ashford where it joined up with the portion from Margate. The evening return working from Ashford to Ramsgate also remained in the HAs' hands.

Royalty were again travellers on the 'Golden Arrow' from Dover to London. On 19 July No E5020 headed the train as it brought Sheikh Rashid bin Saeed al Maktum of Dubai to the capital.

No E5008 was involved in a serious incident on 10 September 1963. It was working the 11:20am Dover Marine to Hither Green Continental 'ferry van' train when most of the vans became derailed between Longfield and Farningham Road. The train of 24 vans parted between the first and second van and a number of the others derailed. The locomotive's automatic brake failed to operate and it was a further 1¼ miles before it stopped under the driver's control.

The derailment's exact cause was never established fully. The inquiry held afterwards determined that the weight of the train had been under-calculated and that the train was travelling at a speed higher than the authorised limit. A series of test runs were held to determine the train's speed at the point of the derailment although both factors were not thought to be significant. The most likely explanation was that some lateral play between the bodies and axles of the ferry vans would allow oscillation to take place if the train was not under traction or buffing. This is the condition which would have applied to the train at the foot of the incline with the power regulator a little open. Colonel W. P. Reed who conducted the inquiry could only assume that the wagons were travelling in the loosest condition and that the variations in cant helped an oscillation to develop which caused the van to become derailed. As a result of the accident modifications were made to the class's braking system. The investigation found that when the train derailed and separated, the automatic brake failed to operate and so bring the locomotive to a halt.

The Southern Region conducted a series of wheelslip tests between Stewarts Lane and Ramsgate on 23 October 1963 with No E5013 hauling four 4CEP units. This was part of a programme of investigative work which lasted into 1964, seeking not only reliability improvements to the class, but also having the requirements of the impending Bournemouth electrification scheme in mind. Full details of these tests and the modifications made to the class are covered in Chapter 6.

The use of the HAs on Royal Trains and other prestige duties was not particularly common and unfortunately on one of those rare occasions, No E5007 disgraced itself. This occurred on 18 November 1963, with the engine chosen to work the special train for the President of Iceland between Gatwick Airport and Victoria. Unfortunately, whilst making its way down to Gatwick with the three empty Pullman cars it failed, and the standby locomotive BRCW Type 3 diesel No D6529 had to be used in its place.

No E5008 stands at Dover Marine with the 'Golden Arrow'. The locomotive is in unlined green and has been fitted with cab rain strips, which would indicate a time after the spring of 1963. The number of Pullman cars in the train would indicate that the picture dates from before May 1965 when second class Pullman cars were removed from the train and ordinary stock substituted. *Class 47 Preservation Project Archive*

Even so the reliability and availability of the class during this period continued to be good. Figures show that in the week ending 2 November, 22 out of the 24 locomotives were available for use. One locomotive was awaiting entry to Eastleigh works and another was already there undergoing attention. This gave an availability figure of 91.3%.

It was a similar story at the end of the month, week ending 30 November. Then there were 21 of the 24 locomotives available, one was not being used and of the other two again one locomotive was awaiting entry to Eastleigh works and another was already there undergoing attention.

Towards the end of the year, one class member found itself hauling a somewhat valuable consignment. On 23 November a collection of Goya masterpieces was carried in a train otherwise mostly loaded with tomatoes from Europe.

A final set of availability figures from the week ending 21 December showed that 21 of the 24 locomotives were available for use, one locomotive was not being used and that the final two were at a depot undergoing attention. During that week those 21 locomotives ran 29,033 miles in service.

The locomotives' mileage between repairs was recorded on the weekly returns prepared by Eastleigh works from their introduction up to the end of 1963. This gives us an opportunity to calculate the average mileage of those locomotives which passed through the works during this period. These figures are similar to those mentioned in S. B. Warder's periodic CEE report to the BRB from November 1964. In it he said the class were averaging around 60,000 miles per locomotive per annum. Their casualty rate was one every 10,000 miles.

Their haulage capacity was tested even further when the Southern Region authorities decided to add two additional vehicles to the 'Night Ferry'. This meant a train of 19 carriages and increased the weight to 850 tons. In other developments, the January 1964 issue of *Railway Magazine* reported that their future use on some commuter trains was being considered. Whilst booked to be hauled by an HA locomotive, there were also occasions when the 'Golden Arrow' was not electrically-hauled. On 14 January 1964 no electric locomotive available and so the down service was entrusted to BRCW Type 3 No D6524.

On 9 April 1964 No E5008 was borrowed by the Central Division and used in place of the usual Co-Co electric locomotive on the 5.14pm Newhaven Harbour to Victoria boat train, two of the three Co-Co electric locomotives being at Eastleigh and undergoing overhauls at the time. The train was double-headed with the HA and 'Standard 5' steam locomotive No 73115, the latter used to provide steam heating for the train.

Just a few days later, No E5009 was involved in a bizarre incident at Petts Wood on 13 April 1964. The locomotive was hauling the 'Golden Arrow', when unbeknown to the train crew, the pantograph raised itself and struck a footbridge. In consequence the pantograph was dislodged and landed on the third-rail. As a result of this incident, an overheight device was fitted to prevent a recurrence. Quite separately and unrelated, the following month No E5002 was seen without its pantograph when working a Brighton to Plymouth service. Running without a pantograph was not unknown although locomotives in such a condition would be restricted to duties such as the 'Golden Arrow' or the 'Night Ferry' where the use of a pantograph would not be required.

The Class HAs continued to make occasional appearances on the Central Division. On 20 December 1964 No E5005 was used on the 11.00 Eastbourne to Brighton service.

Locomotive Utilisation 1959-1963

Loco No	Months Recorded Mileage	No. Works Visits	Recorded Mileage	Ave Monthly Mileage
E5000/E5024	46	2	190,571	4,143
E5001	24	1	102,116	4,255
E5002	19	1	52,250	2,764
E5003	22	1	70,772	3,217
E5004	18	1	68,180	3,788
E5005	48	2	229,828	4,788
E5006	44	1	250,678	5,697
E5007	50	0	187,081	3,742
E5008	45	1	139,872	3,108
E5009	44	1	156,967	3,567
E5010	49	1	222,935	4,550
E5011	30	0	105,559	3,518
E5012	32	0	109,160	3,411
E5013	16	0	59,007	3,688
E5017	10	0	30,844	3,084
E5018	34	2	130,988	3,853
E5020	32	0	114,135	3,567
E5021	36	1	136,637	3,796

The BR CME J. F. Harrison submitted a memorandum on 8 January 1965 to the Works & Equipment Committee and the Main Workshops Committee for additional spare parts for the 24 HA locomotives and the three Co-Co electric locomotives. At the time of Harrison writing, BR held spares worth £44,000 and he was now looking to purchase an additional £50,000 worth of parts for both types. This purchase was authorised on 16 February.

Another occasion when diesel traction was used in place of the regular electric locomotive was on the 'Night Ferry' on 5 March 1965. Such was the weight of the train by this time that two BRCW Type 3 locomotives, Nos D6517 and D6524, were used instead of the usual single electric locomotive for the journey to Victoria.

The regular summer departure time for the 'Night' Ferry from London was 10pm. On 11 May however, the train's departure was delayed, awaiting the arrival of Barbara Castle MP, the Minister for Overseas Development. She was travelling to Paris on Government business; a recent sinus operation meant flying was not an option. At the time the Government's majority was just three so the train was held so she could vote in a 10pm division at the House of Commons. Not surprisingly, when word slipped out a few weeks later, questions were asked in the very same Parliament. In answers given, it transpired however that this was not the first time the Southern Region had been asked to hold the train to assist travelling Government ministers. Back in June 1962 for example, the 'Night Ferry' was held for 30 minutes at Dover at Home Secretary R. A. Butler's request as he returned from holiday.

The prestige of the 'Golden Arrow' was reduced somewhat from 30 May 1965 onwards when the second class Pullman cars were withdrawn from the formation and in their place ordinary BR second class coaches used. From then on only four first class Pullman cars remained in the formation.

The timetable change came on 14 June and was notable in that it was the first to use the 24 hour clock. It was also the last timetable where all 24 HA locomotives were in service. Aside from the two main passenger trains, there were 10 parcels duties allocated to them; several of these, as with previous years, originated in London. There was also one very short parcels train. It started with a light engine movement from Rochester to Chatham, booked journey time three minutes. On arrival the locomotive was then used on the 19:45 parcels train to Gillingham, arrival time 19:48.

On Sundays there was far less work for the class, the early morning parcels and newspaper trains were mainly worked by the region's BRCW Type 3 diesels, other than the 04:00 Victoria to Dover Priory service. Their only non-freight duties were the 'Night Ferry' and 'Golden Arrow' services, the daily service between Wolverhampton and the Kent coast was discontinued, in which the HAs had been used to work the portion between Ashford and Ramsgate in both directions. During the week there was also now only one relief available to the 'Night Ferry' from Dover Marine each morning compared to two in previous years although two relief trains could be run on weekends leaving Dover Marine at 07:50 and 08:08 respectively. Both were booked to be HA hauled.

The freight timetable introduced at the same time saw the locomotives continue to be active across the South Eastern Division. Hither Green, Dover, Ashford, and Tonbridge all saw a steady procession of Class HA locomotives each day. As with previous years, Sundays were very quiet with only a handful of freight duties for them, though there was provision for several services between Dover Marine and Hither Green Continental Depot if demand required them.

On 11 September 1965 the 'Night Ferry' train was waiting at Dover Docks to carry the night's travellers from the continent to London when there was an explosion in the dining car with the result that four men were injured. It was thought to have been caused by a gas leak in the train kitchen.

The 'Night Ferry' through the 1960s continued to be a stern test for the HA locomotives. A. G. S. Davies writing in *Railway World* in December 1980 described a journey made on the train from Dover to London in September 1965. The make-up of the train included six sleeping cars and seven ordinary carriages, with a gross weight of 650 tons. With No E5006 in charge, the departure from Dover was nine minutes late, but a spirited run ensued. The speed up the bank at Shepherdswell was 48mph and the train then accelerated down the hill to Bekesbourne passing there at 80mph. The speed on Ensden bank increased from 34mph when coming off the curve at Canterbury A junction to 48½mph at the summit. Faversham was reached in just 34 minutes with a passing speed recorded of 75mph. Chatham was passed in 52½ minutes with a top speed on the stretch from Faversham of 68mph near Sittingbourne. The curve at Rochester bridge, meant slowing to 25mph but the train's speed then increased to 48mph at Sole Street, which was passed in 64 minutes. This represented a gain on the scheduled time of some six minutes. No E5006 had a clear road ahead and reached 87mph at Farningham Road. Swanley summit was topped at 65mph, and St Mary Cray was passed at 71mph. This meant Bickley was passed in 77 minutes. A clear road was maintained through the south London suburbs giving an arrival at Victoria 98¾ minutes after leaving Dover Marine, a commendable 12-minute gain on the 110-minute schedule the train was timetabled for.

A new freight timetable for the Southern Region came into operation on 4 October 1965 and with minimal change involved. Of these there were a number of alterations to individual services and their timings but overall the level of work for the Class HA locomotives was basically the same as compared to the previous timetable introduced four months earlier. During the duration of this timetable however, withdrawals would start of some Class HA locomotives, so they could be converted to electro-diesels for the Bournemouth scheme.

It is noticeable when going through this timetable that there were a growing number of duties that were allocated to the Class JB electro-diesels that were starting to be delivered from English Electric. The first of these were starting to arrive just as this timetable came into use. It was their introduction that enabled the Class HA withdrawals.

The 1965 'National Traction Plan' was compiled using standardised criteria. These included future mileage taking into account the implementation of the Reshaping Plan ('Beeching Axe'), freight and coal concentration plans and the freight sundries plan. The second factor considered was the present speed of services with a target increase of up to 15% being sought. Thirdly there was the load of freight trains, with an increase in payload required. Finally locomotive utilisation was to be assumed to be twelve hours a day – the availability of the 24 HA electric locomotives was assumed to be 90%. The overall formula used was to multiply the average future speed by 12 hours, and dividing this figure into the total future mileage.

The plan showed that as at December 1964, the Southern Region had assessed they had a surplus of 10 HA locomotives, all of which were to be converted to electro-diesels for the forthcoming Bournemouth electrification scheme. The first example to be taken out of service for conversion was No E5015 which was towed to Crewe in January 1966.

Part of the reason for the surplus was the arrival of the JB electro-diesel locomotives. An early sign of their arrival onto the HAs' territory was on 17 December 1965 when No E6010, only delivered the previous month, was seen passing Faversham on a freight duty.

Kent was hit badly by blizzards in the middle of January 1966. One feature of which was that during the worst of the weather, on 17 and 20 January, the 'Night Ferry' was double-headed by two BRCW Type 3 diesels rather than the usual HA electric locomotive.

A few days later, on 28 January 1966, a strange cavalcade was seen heading to Eastleigh. Electro-diesel No E6004 was hauling HA electric locomotive No E5010 and BRCW Type 3 diesel No D6526. The ensemble travelled via Brighton and along the south coast.

The South-Eastern Division suffered major disruption on 24 March 1966. That day, No E5012 was working the 14:40 Hither Green to Hoo Junction freight service. Shortly after departure it became derailed blocking the Lee spur for some 12 hours.

On 16 May, all of the Southern Region's cross channel ferry services were stopped as a result of the national seaman's strike. Consequently, some boat train services including the 'Golden Arrow' were suspended for the duration of the dispute and the region's shipping services did not resume until 2 July. The suspension of the 'Golden Arrow' proved fortunate as a shunting incident on 13 June at Clapham Junction caused minor damage to some 'Bournemouth Belle' Pullman cars. The seamen's dispute thus meant that the 'Golden Arrow' stock could be used on the 'Bournemouth Belle'. Hence, the following day the 'Bournemouth Belle' was formed partly of its usual stock and partly of 'Golden Arrow' stock.

Over the years, the HA type were used on several enthusiast railtours. The Locomotive Club of Great Britain (LCGB) in conjunction with *Railway Magazine* ran several tours to destinations in France between 1965 and 1967. The 'Pas de Calais' tour of 30 May 1965 used No E5020 for the first part of the journey between Charing Cross and Folkestone Junction Siding. The following year, for 'The Somme Railtour' run on 15 May, No E5005 was provided for the return journey between Folkestone East Yard and Victoria, running via Ashford and Tonbridge. Almost exactly a year later on 14 May 1967, the 'Calais-Lille Railtour' was run. This time No E5007 was used to take participants from Victoria to Folkestone.

New electro-diesel No E6025 was used on the afternoon Hoo Junction to Dover Town freight service on 8 June in place of the usual HA electric locomotive. However, at Faversham it exchanged trains with HA No E5019 which had arrived on a Dover Marine to Hither Green freight service.

There was a further accident involving an HA locomotive hauling a ferry van train on 27 July 1966. At 15:58 No E5002 left Hither Green (Continental Depot) heading for Dover Marine. The train was made up of 24 empty ferry vans and a brake van. Much of the train was vacuum braked though this was inoperative on the fourth and eighth vehicles. The train derailed about a mile outside Sittingbourne on the London side, with the rear 18 vans and the brake van coming off the rails. The locomotive and the first six vans remained on the track. These were undamaged. The train divided between the seventh and eighth vehicles. The track was badly damaged and normal working did not resume until 29 July.

As part of the investigation into the accident, a test run was made using No E5002 with a similar train to find out what speed would be achieved at the point of derailment if the driver controlled it as the driver involved in the accident had stated in his evidence. This was arranged by Mr. J. F. Rogers the Divisional Movements Manager, South Eastern Division, on 30 August. The driver was instructed to maintain 45mph. subject to the observance of more severe speed restrictions, until approaching Bobbing Bank where the speed was to be 38mph. The train was then to be allowed to coast freely until it became necessary to control it.

As a result of these tests the inquiry determined that the train was likely to have been travelling at around 60mph; compared to the permitted maximum of 45mph. Imperfections in the track enhanced the swing of the vans causing most likely the seventh van to derail. Had the train been travelling slower, the oscillation at that point probably would not have caused the derailment. (See also p79 of *Southern Way Special issue No 13: The Other Side of the Southern – Accidents, Incidents and Occasions Part 2*.)

The following month, August, the class were reallocated en bloc to Ashford Chart Leacon from Stewarts Lane. Those that remained as straight electric locomotives would now be allocated there for the rest of their service lives. This move coincided with the introduction of a new freight timetable. By now the first three locomotives had been moved to Crewe for conversion to electro-diesels.

The level of work for the Class JB electro-diesels is again noteworthy. When looking at this timetable in some detail there are some freight services that were previously worked by the Class HA locomotives which were now in the hands of these new locomotives and with most of the Class JBs having entered service by now. An example was the early morning 03:45 Ashford to Brookgate Sidings, retimed from 02:15, which had become electro-diesel worked, as was the case with the 12:10 Dover Town to Faversham.

The HAs were seen on a number of cross London freight services, with Longhedge Junction the usual changeover point. The 16:10 Ashford to Willesden and 16:45 Ashford to Temple Mills were a case in point. Going the other way, one of the Feltham to Ashford services saw the Class JB electro-diesel give way to a Class HA there.

On Saturdays, the 16:15 Dover Marine to Hither Green Continental, which previously had been a conditional service, now ran each Saturday. Sunday work for the class was again very small, in keeping with previous years.

On 13 September 1966 JA electro-diesel No E6012 was used on the 'Golden Arrow' from Victoria. The two and half weeks between 31 October and 17 November saw the 'Golden Arrow' diverted to Folkestone as there was dredging work being undertaken in Dover Harbour. Notwithstanding the test earlier, the HAs were banned from the Folkestone Harbour branch and so electro-diesels were used instead.

On the 21 December the 'Night Ferry' to Victoria hauled by No E5004 was running so late that it was passed at Petts Wood by the 'Golden Arrow' heading in the opposite direction hauled by No E5013. Based on the timetable in operation at that time, this would have meant the 'Night Ferry' would have been running around 90 minutes to the bad.

A failure of No E5011 on 18 April 1967 whilst working the London bound 'Night Ferry' caused all manner of chaos as the 17-coach train was stranded between Canterbury East and Faversham. Despite the weight of the train (likely 800-plus tons), JB electro-diesel No E6028 was sent from Canterbury and was able to propel the stranded train to Faversham. After No E5011 had been removed from the train by electro-diesel No E6049, it and No E6028 were then used to take the train to London, leaving Faversham at about 9:43am.

BR availability statistics from the time show that on 7 June 1967 there were 24 locomotives for 11 diagrams. Eleven locomotives were diagrammed for work but the other 13 were shown as 'unavailable'. On that basis it would give an availability figure for the class of 45.8%. What these figures do not say is that 10 of the 'unavailable' 13 locomotives were at Crewe undergoing conversion to electro-diesel locomotives. If the figures are recalculated on the basis of 11 out of 14 locomotives being available for traffic then their availability would have been 78.5%. Even with this level of availability, things could and did go wrong for example when on the 27 June No E5022 failed whilst working a Hither Green to Ashford Class 7 freight.

The new freight timetable came into operation across the region on 10 July 1967 and with it the end of steam working throughout. On this occasion there were some major differences from previous years, one of the most notable being the introduction of air-braked freight services on the South Eastern Division. Of these new trains, a number were booked to be worked by HA locomotives. For the HAs the main services were the Ferry wagon trains to and from Dover Marine and Hither Green, as well as a car-transporter train which originated at Knowle and Dorridge in the West Midlands, leaving there at 23:00. This working, previously a JB electro-

The HAs were not regular visitors to Charing Cross. However No E5020 is captured there on 30 May 1965 as it waits to leave with the LCGB's 'Pas de Calais' railtour. *Class 47 Preservation Project Archive*

No E5013 leaves Ashford with a train of oil tankers taking power from the overhead wire system there. In the background is one of the JA electro-diesels.
Class 47 Preservation Project Archive

diesel duty, consisted of 20 car flats of British Motor Corporation (BMC) cars for export. An HA was booked to take over the train at Longhedge Junction, heading down to Dover Town at 03:41 and operated Monday to Saturdays. On Sundays there were just the two air-braked services from Dover to Hither Green for the HAs.

The new passenger timetable started the same day. With 10 of the HA locomotives now at Crewe to be converted to electro-diesels, there was a noticeable reduction in the number of services allocated to the remaining 14. Even so the booked time for the 'Night Ferry' leaving Victoria at 22:00 was 88 minutes to Dover which represented a small acceleration compared to previously. The 'winter' season started on 20 October and continued until 15 March 1968. Departure time then was an hour earlier from Victoria at 21:00. The Up working to London left Dover at 07:20 as per usual. This train had a relief service available, also booked to be hauled by a HA locomotive which as with previous timetables left at 07:50. A second relief train was available at weekends, leaving Dover Marine at 08.08, and this too was booked for a Class HA locomotive if it was required.

The early hours of the morning would see members of the class active on several parcel, passenger, and newspaper trains. There were two departures from Victoria, one at 03.00 to Ramsgate carrying passengers, parcels and newspapers, the second to Dover Marine at 03.40 carrying passengers and newspapers. In addition there was a parcels duty from Southwark to Ramsgate leaving at 02.30. The class also had several daytime parcels duties as well as two empty stock workings, one from Margate at 09.25, the other from Dover Marine at 10.35, both for Bricklayers Arms.

Saturdays were a similar picture to weekdays for both passenger and parcels duties. In contrast, on Sundays their work was purely the 'Night Ferry' and 'Golden Arrow' in both directions and the two 'Night Ferry' relief trains from Dover as and when required routed via Sevenoaks.

Another van train was involved in an accident on 17 July 1967. That day No E5010 was hauling the 15.28 Class 5 goods from Ashford to Willesden. The train was made up of 26 loaded continental ferry wagons and a brake van. The incident happened on a falling gradient when No E5010 failed to stop and collided at about 15mph with the rear of the 15.24 Maidstone East–Victoria passenger service made up of two 2HAP EMUs. The causes were identified as a combination of the Guard who had prepared the train failing to ensure it had a 'fitted head' of at least 14 vehicles and miscalculating the train's weight, and the third factor was excessive speed by the driver. Had the train been running at the correct speed, the inquiry determined that the accident would not have happened despite the other identified deficiencies. (See also p63 of *Southern Way Special issue No 13: The Other Side of the Southern – Accidents, Incidents and Occasions Part 2*.)

The make-up of the 'Night Ferry' was revised for the 1967-68 winter sports season, with in late December the provision of a sleeping car running through from London to Basle in Switzerland. The same arrangement was made for the 1968-69 season starting on 20 December for the outward journey and a day later for coming to London. The service finished with the 28 February departure from London and the 1 March return from Basle.

A further set of availability statistics dated 14 February 1968 give a more accurate picture. There were 11 locomotives for 11 diagrams, with three locomotives listed as unavailable. This gave a much more accurate figure of 78.6% availability.

Although loadings on the 'Night Ferry' remained heavy, there was concern for the future. As a result fare reductions were made starting from 1 March 1968 and which led to a welcome increase in passenger numbers of over 30%. This compared with previous years where sleeping car passengers had fallen from 50,982 in 1960 to 39,987 in 1965. Overall passenger numbers had remained healthy but with a rise in the number of foot passengers from 48,080 in 1960 to 89,306 in 1965.

The LCGB's 'Invicta Railtour' run on 3 March 1968 covered a variety of lines in Kent. The soon to be re-numbered No E5022 was used on the leg from Plumstead to Victoria via Slade Green, Bexleyheath, Lewisham, and Nunhead. Unfortunately at Slade Green, the locomotive became gapped on the third-rail and stalled and with in this instance the booster equipment unable to move the locomotive. According to reports a 4EPB multiple-unit used to move the train resulted in a 45-minute delay.

The next passenger timetable change came on 6 May 1968. There was a minor re-timing in the Working Timetable of the 'Night Ferry' departure from Dover to leave at 07.22, although it was still shown in the public book as leaving at 07.20. During the week there was one relief train available leaving Dover at 08.05 and arriving at Victoria at 09.38. Again as in previous years this was sent via Sevenoaks. Whereas previously there had been winter and summer departure times from London for both the 'Golden Arrow' and 'Night Ferry' this timetable saw just the one time used throughout the year. For the 'Golden Arrow' this was 10.30 from Victoria, returning from Dover at 18.13. The 'Night Ferry' was booked to leave Victoria at 22:00 each night.

On Sunday there was an earlier relief train available if required, leaving Dover at 07.52 as per previous timetables. These trains along with the 'Night Ferry' proper and 'Golden Arrow' services were again the HAs only non-freight work on a Sunday. The early morning newspaper and parcels trains, a feature of the HAs duties since their introduction, changed over to diesel haulage. With engineering work a common occurrence on a Sunday and the consequential loss of traction current, it was perhaps an inevitable move. Similarly the 11.00 empty stock working from Ramsgate to Bricklayers Arms was now diesel-hauled.

The freight timetable also changed on 6 May. There were very few changes when compared to the previous one. The levels of work remained unchanged, with the air-braked Dover to Hither Green services being some of their most important work. On the 09.35 Sunday departure from Dover they were booked to run in just 1 hour and 28 minutes.

Notwithstanding the conductor rail then extending west as far as Bournemouth, the class only occasionally found their way to the South Western Division and again mainly when they were heading to and from Eastleigh for, or following, works attention. However, on 12 June 1968 No E5010 was used on a Guildford to Margate special throughout. A South Western Division conductor was used on the section of the journey from Guildford to Clapham Junction.

The overall freight situation on the Southern Region in 1968 was not good. The returns for the first 33 weeks of the year (up to 17 August) showed a £540,000 decrease of receipts as compared to the same time in 1967. The region cited several reasons for this but generally there was a shortage of available locomotives in the early part of the year which had affected the movement of loads. This had ongoing repercussions as several parcels companies were taking their traffic to other regions' London termini.

In terms of wagon load losses, the main factors identified were the Elders-Fyffes banana traffic where less wagons were needed following their switch from stems to cartons, and the reduction of canned goods passing through Southampton. On the South Eastern Division, there was a significant drop in paper products moved by rail as Kimberley-Clark Ltd had switched much of their distribution to road transport.

Another member of the class to stray from its usual area was No E5008, which on 6 October was noted stabled at Selhurst depot on the Central Division.

Towards the end of 1968, a tidying up exercise of locomotive numbers was carried out following the conversion of 10 to become Class 74s hence there were a number of gaps in the number series. As a result on 13 October No E5022 became No E5006 and No E5020 became No E5005. Later on 15 December, No E5018 was renumbered to No E5003. As a result the number series was now E5001 to No E5014.

The work from the 1965 'National Traction Plan' was developed further and in December 1968 an updated plan was published. This gave a revised forecast of BR's locomotive requirements up to 1974 and had been prepared in November 1967. The 1965 plan had required updating as many statistics had become out of date and new standards for locomotive utilisation and availability had been set. These measures were based both on the latest information available and operating experience gained since 1965.

Page 15 of the 1968 'National Traction Plan' detailed the Southern Region's electric locomotive fleet as at 5 October 1968. In addition to the three Southern Railway Co-Co locomotives the region had 49 Class 73 electro-diesels along with 14 Class 71 straight electric locomotives and 10 Class 74 electro-diesels. The forecast stock at year-end between 1968 and 1974 showed that the region would retain its entire electric and electro-diesel locomotive stock. Availability targets were also given: for the Class 71s for 1969 and 1970 it was set at 75%, and for the Class 74s it was 70% in 1969 rising to 80% in 1970.

A new freight timetable was introduced on 6 January 1969 and with the main Class 71 duties remaining substantially the same when compared to the May 1968 timetable. The expansion of the Freightliner network also saw the class booked to work the 01.15 Dover Marine to Stratford (Mondays excepted) as far as Hither Green. The air-braked Dover Marine to Hither Green Continental Depot services were all booked to complete their journeys in less than two hours. The only one of these services not to manage this was the 08.10 from Dover which was allowed 2 hours 7 minutes. One addition to their work in this timetable was the weekday 16.30 freight from Richborough to Hoo Junction.

A further report based on the freight returns for the week ending 18 January 1969 reinforced the problems being encountered by the Southern Region. The South Eastern Division had a planned freight mileage that week of 29,565 miles, of which only 88%, some 25,962 miles, were run. The South Western Division by comparison had planned to run 32,694 miles but had only achieved 81% of that figure, 26,401 miles. This meant that the South Eastern Division loading were only 72% of what had been planned and 85% the South Western Division had planned. Again both measures of actual miles run and loadings were showing a sizable drop when compared to those from 1967.

On 18 February No E5006 failed between Margate and Herne Bay whilst working the 19.15 Margate to Hither Green freight service. Two 4CEP units were used to push the train into the Up loop at Herne Bay. A Class 73 took the freight train onto Faversham with No E5006 being hauled dead.

There were two further Class 71 failures reported during March. On 11 March the locomotive used on a Victoria to Ramsgate newspaper train failed at Slade Green. The train was 165 minutes late by the time it reached Herne Bay. Then on 23 March the locomotive used on the 'Golden Arrow' failed at Longfield. As a consequence, arrival at Dover was 198 minutes late.

Over at Eastleigh works, on 12 April No E5012 was seen there undergoing an overhaul.

The new timetable came into operation on 5 May 1969. The freight timetable showed some changes when compared to the one from January. The afternoon freight working from Richborough was discontinued and the use of the Class 71s on the 01.15 Dover to Stratford Freightliner also came to an end.

No E5006 with the 'Golden Arrow' at Dover Marine. This is not, however, the original locomotive that carried this number but the former No E5022 which was renumbered as part of a 'tidying up' exercise in late 1968, the original No E5006 having been converted to a Class 74 electro-diesel.
Class 47 Preservation Project Archive

A Class 71 hauled 'Golden Arrow' in the late 1960s. The Class 71 carries the headboard and flags, though the body mounted arrows had fallen into disuse by now. The train's four Pullman cars are in the two styles of blue and grey livery, the reversed version being short-lived.
Class 47 Preservation Project Archive

The other key alterations to the Class 71s' work concerned the Knowle & Dorridge car transporter train where the locomotive changeover point was moved from Longhedge Junction to Ashford for the journey to Dover. The return working to the West Midlands was diesel-hauled throughout. On the plus side, the Monday to Saturday 20.00 North Camp to Hoo Junction freight was Class 71 hauled from Tonbridge Yard.

With the passenger timetable there were several noteworthy changes. Whereas in previous years the 'Golden Arrow' and 'Night Ferry' had both had separate winter and summer departure times, this timetable saw both trains have a single departure time throughout the year. The 'Golden Arrow' was timetabled to leave Victoria at 10.30 returning from Dover Marine at 18.13. The 'Night Ferry' departure time was also fixed: 22.00 from Victoria and 07.20 from Dover.

A new working for the class was the 20.40 Dover to Willesden mail train which they worked as far as Tonbridge. On the debit side, the 05.03 Faversham to Dover passenger, and newspaper train, which had been a Class 71 duty for many years now became a Class 73 duty instead. Similarly, the morning ECS train from Margate to Bricklayers Arms became a Class 73 duty where previously it had been Class 71 worked.

Whilst test trains involving the newly-converted Class 74s on the South Western Division during 1968 and 1969 were commonplace, the use of a Class 71 was decidedly unusual. However on 15 June 1969 No E5006 was used to haul two 4VEP EMUs from Waterloo to Eastleigh. Such a load was the same as many of the Class 74 test trains then being operated.

On 2 September 1969 a Class 71 hauled freight service derailed at Sittingbourne. The train, comprised of eight empty Fruit D vans, was travelling at 65mph when the rear vehicle came off the rails. The subsequent investigation found that the cause was due to lateral oscillation of the vans of considerable magnitude in an area of low rail joints.

The pathing of the 'Night Ferry' from Dover to London was always a problem for the timetable planners particularly on weekdays, when because of its unreliability in arrival at the Kent port, it still had to be fitted in with the intensive commuter service. For example, at Chatham in the late 1960s, there was only a four-minute gap for the train behind the 07.02 Ramsgate to Victoria semi-fast service. This problem was demonstrated in a run published in the November 1969 *Railway World*. The train load was 590 tons, a lesser load than the early years of the Class 71s on this train. On this particular journey Faversham was passed in 38¼ minutes, but followed by a permanent way slack of 20mph and some signal checks with Chatham being passed 59 minutes after leaving Dover. There was some lively running after Chatham and 81mph was recorded when passing at Farningham Road. Bickley Junction was reached in 83¾ minutes. As previously, threading the train through the morning rush hour proved a challenge and Victoria was reached in 113¼ minutes.

5
Livery Changes

Above: **Standing at Dover Marine in charge of the 'Golden Arrow' is No E5012 in October 1967. The locomotive carries one of the several variants of small yellow warning panel applied to these locomotives. Alongside is a BRCW Type 3 diesel, one of the 12 built to the Hastings line gauge. It too has a small yellow panel, though the Southern Region were particularly slow compared to others to apply this warning device.**

Unlined Green

After all the discussion regarding the locomotives' livery the scheme decided upon did not last long. As early as 9 June 1961 Mr Sykes was writing to the Assistant General Manager David McKenna about the HA's livery. He said that due to some deficiencies in the original paint used at Doncaster it had been necessary to repaint some locomotives. No E5004 had been one of these and the repainting took place after its overhaul at Eastleigh in May 1961. When repainted, the red and white lining had been omitted as it was thought it slightly improved the appearance. Sykes continued by saying that his department had been in contact with Misha Black, who had prepared the locomotives' original livery, and he had no strong feelings about the lining band and its retention. As Mr McKenna had been involved in the original livery discussions, Sykes thought it only right he should know that it was now planned to omit the lining band if Mr McKenna had no objection.

David McKenna replied three days later. He had come to London that morning on the 'Night Ferry' and had seen one of the newly-painted locomotives without the lining and thought it looked very well. He would have no objection to it being omitted in future. As a result, from this point onwards, locomotives were given unlined green following overhauls at Eastleigh.

Yellow Warning Panels and Other Changes

The BTC's Operating Committee decided on 3 July 1959 to commission a series of visibility tests. The purpose was to determine if locomotives and multiple-units with distinctive markings would aid trackside staff. Following the tests, and involving several types of marking and stock, the British Railway Sub-Commission on 23 July 1961 decided that yellow warning panels should be adopted as standard. The shape of the panel was to be devised by the Design Panel for each locomotive type.

Some examples gained the small yellow warning panel on the cab front. However of all the BR regions the Southern comes across in various documents as being quite sceptical as to the value of such a policy and how it should be applied. Their arguments were set out in a memorandum on the subject dated 20 July 1962. In their view they were not convinced of the usefulness of such a panel, allied to the fact that the panels would need to be kept clean.

As a result a number of the HA type ran for a number of years after 1962 still in full green livery and without a yellow warning panel of any shape or size. Indeed, both Nos E5003 and E5005 still had not been given a yellow panel by the time they were taken to Crewe for rebuilding as electro-diesel locomotives. No E5024 was another locomotive to be sent to Crewe in 1966 for conversion without having received a small yellow panel. By comparison No E5017 had been given a small yellow panel by the time it arrived at Crewe for conversion.

The size of this panel on the HA type varied with the known main variations summarised below.

In the years immediately before the introduction of BR blue, the green used was also changed from carriage green to standard locomotive green, a much darker shade.

Following the further change in BR policy in 1966, some of the class, No E5010 being one, gained a full yellow front. The guinea-pig locomotive for this livery style was No E5023. This was given a full yellow panel and inspected by BR's Industrial Design team in August 1966. The Head of Accident Prevention at BR was particularly keen to see full yellow ends applied to all locomotives as soon as possible and raised this with the recently appointed Chief Engineer (Traction and Rolling Stock) (CE [T&RS]) A. E. Robson in February 1967. His request was duly passed onto BR Workshops within days. However, the application of any type of yellow panel on the HAs continued to be somewhat random; by March 1968 for example No E5002 was still in all over green.

No E5004 stabled at Faversham. The locomotive was the first of the class to emerge from an overhaul at Eastleigh in unlined green.
Class 47 Preservation Project Archive

Corporate BR Blue

May 1964 saw the launch of BR's new corporate image and with it a new locomotive livery. The first moves towards a new livery for the HA electric locomotives came in late 1965. A series of locomotive drawings, including one of the HA locomotives, was sent to Ted Wilkes of the design consultants Wilkes, Ashmore Ltd on 19 November 1965. Wilkes' task was to determine the new blue livery for each class including the location of the new BR symbol. Wilkes had been used before to assist with livery details, most notably in 1962 working on the livery for the Brush Type 4s. He returned the drawings at the end of November with his thoughts included.

HA locomotives Yellow Warning Panel Variations – A Summary

Locomotive No	Yellow Warning Panel Type
E5001	2ft 10in deep by 9ft wide, with square top corners, set just below the handrail.
E5012	1ft 9in deep by 8ft wide with rounded upper corners, set just below the handrail.
E5008	
E5009	
E5011	
E5014	
E5017	
E5021	2ft 6in deep by 8ft just above the buffer beam
E5018	
E5022	3ft by 6ft. A rectangle just above the centre of the buffer beam
E5023	Full yellow front carried 6 inches around the cab sides.

No E5009 after arrival at Victoria with the 'Night Ferry' from Dover Marine. The locomotive has the style of small yellow warning panel applied to it and at least five other examples.
Class 47 Preservation Project Archive

No E5013 stabled at Ashford with another member of the class. It shows one of the several variations of small yellow panel the class were given. The other locomotive in the picture is one of only a handful of examples to gain full yellow ends whilst still in green.
Class 47 Preservation Project Archive

The CE (T&RS) J. F. Harrison sent the first proposals from the Director of Industrial Design to R. G. Jarvis for their new livery. These proposals centred mainly on the position and form of the new BR symbol, the numbers, and the yellow warning panel. At this point blue livery had yet to be approved for existing locomotives, only new ones were so presented, and nothing could be done until that approval was given, which came on 9 June 1966, after which work continued on the new livery and its application over the following months. A memorandum was circulated on 20 December illustrating the Industrial Design Department's basic principles for the new colour scheme. Amongst the types illustrated were the HA electric locomotives.

The first of the HA type to be painted in rail blue with a full yellow end was No E5007. The yellow extended six inches around from the cab fronts and also on to the start of the cab roof. This was to ensure a full yellow front was seen by trackside staff. In addition, the buffer beams were now painted black not red, and the ETH jumper and plug were painted orange not the green body colour used previously. The locomotive number was applied at both ends of the bodyside. Another early recipient of the new colour scheme was No E5004 when it was ex-works from Eastleigh on 15 April 1967. By November that year No E5020 had been given the new livery also.

Classification

Two-digit class numbers were introduced for all BR diesel and electric locomotives in March 1968, the HA Type locomotives becoming the Class 71. Details of the new classifications were circulated by A. E. Robson the CE (T&RS) on 22 March and were to be used forthwith. In his memo, Robson explained that locomotive records, costing and certain casualty and failure data were currently being programmed for computer operation, which had determined the need for this type of numerical code.

No E5007 at Stewart's Lane and freshly painted in BR blue on 1 May 1971. This locomotive was the first of the class to be given the livery. During this period the locomotive numbers were applied to both ends of the bodyside.
Class 47 Preservation Project Archive

Above: **The Up 'Night Ferry' passes Petts Wood near Bromley on the morning of 9 October 1968, with the blue liveried No E5008 in charge. Although the train is still well loaded, only five sleeping cars are in use, a noticeable reduction from only a few years previously.** *J. Cooper-Smith*

Below: **No E5010 was one of a small number of the Class 71s to be given a full yellow warning panel whilst still in green livery. In this condition it waits to leave Victoria on 5 June 1969 with the 'Golden Arrow'.** *John Scrace*

Eastleigh Works

Above: **In company with BRCW Type 3 No D6502, HA electric No E5006 waits to be taken into Eastleigh works for overhaul in 1962. The locomotive is already without a pantograph. The locomotive is in its original livery, something that would be lost when repainted this time around. No E5006 would in time be one of the HAs rebuilt as an electro-diesel, whilst No D6502 was written off following an accident on 5 March 1964 at Itchingfield Junction.**
Class 47 Preservation Project Archive

Below: **No E5020 stands at Eastleigh prior to overhaul. The locomotive is in unlined SR green with no yellow warning panel. The Southern Region was sceptical of the worth of the yellow panel and therefore slow to apply it to their locomotives and multiple-unit stock.**
Class 47 Preservation Project Archive

Eastleigh Works

Above: **A sparkling ex-works No E5020 on 24 February 1963 after completion of an overhaul there. The locomotive is now painted in unlined green and has rainstrips fitted above each cab door.** *Class 47 Preservation Project Archive*

Below: **No E5014 after overhaul at Eastleigh on 20 April 1963.** *Class 47 Preservation Project Archive*

6
Modifications

Above: **A couple of years after entering service, No E5002 is seen at Hither Green. The only noticeable differences from when it left Doncaster are the small headcode characters and the repositioned ETH jumper cable.** *Class 47 Preservation Project Archive*

The HA type electric locomotives underwent a number of modifications during their time in service. Some external and some related to their electrical equipment.

In February 1959, a serious fire damaged the main control cubicle of No E5000 when it was standing in Norwood Yard. The cause was later established as the failure of the main line-switch to clear a small arc when the booster set was idling. This had led to a build-up of electrically conducting ionised gas allowing a power arc to form between the positive terminal and earthed metal causing much damage.

The idling current was only about 70 amps and the line switch was designed to rupture 5,000 amps and could handle up to 20,000 amps. Unfortunately, at very low currents, the magnetisation of the blow out coils was insufficient to quench the arc.

The line-switches were operated electro-pneumatically and closed by energising a small magnetic air valve. The simple solution was to direct the magnet valve exhaust, when it was de-energised, between the main contacts to produce an air blast which thus cleared the arc.

Voltage variation on the third rail due to other trains is normal. When the booster set is idling, its back E.M.F tended to remain more or less constant. To prevent the set feeding back into the third rail when the third rail voltage fell below the booster set voltage a polarised current relay detected this and opened the line switch. This was the explanation for the low current. The line switch would be re-closed when the booster set voltage had fallen to about 15% below the third rail voltage.

The booster sets fitted in the first two locomotives had duplex wave windings. Due to current imbalance between the two armature windings there were problems with commutation. As a result, the windings were soon changed to the more conventional lap windings for the other locomotives and those on the first two were changed to match.

The first visible change made was during construction. From No E5006 onwards metal kickplates were fitted below the cab doors and using a similar material to that used in the equipment room. The first six locomotives however remained unaltered during their working lives.

Two further changes made early on, indeed quite visible ones at that, were the relocation of the ETH jumper cable from the cab front to a position on the buffer beam, behind the locomotive's left-hand buffer. Locomotives from the second batch were built with the jumper cable in the revised position.

The second change was to the two-digit roller blind headcode. When built, the numerals and letters on the blinds

The revised grille arrangement as fitted to both Nos 71004 and 71011 is clear to see in this view of No 71011, stabled at Ashford, when compared with classmate No 71003 which retained the original arrangement. *Class 47 Preservation Project Archive*

were the same size as the stencil type used on much of the region's EMU fleet at the time, 16in x 6in. With the need identified for the region's diesel and electric locomotives to display a headcode that included both numbers and letters, a redesign was required so as to fit in all the additional information. If the existing character size had been retained, longer blinds would have been required, with a consequential alteration of the mechanism. In September 1959, a series of tests were carried out on the legibility of smaller characters 9in x 6in. Whilst they were less visible to staff by around 30 to 40 yards, overall the tests determined that staff found the smaller numerals more visible. As a result multiple–units were changed to blinds with the smaller type as were the HA electric locomotives. No E5004 was one locomotive changed very early on and had the smaller character blinds by July 1960, as were Nos E5000 and E5001.

The test runs carried out in the autumn of 1959 from Victoria to Dover, enabled a simple wheelslip protection device to be developed and fitted to the whole class to overcome the armature overspeed problem. Differential current relays were fitted to measure any current differences between the parallel pairs of motors, caused by one of the motors slipping. When one of these relays operated, the control camshaft would run back to reduce power until the slipping was controlled. The anti-slip brake was simultaneously automatically applied to slow down the slipping wheels. Locomotive No E5009 was the first to be fitted with this system, it was reasonably effective but was still far from being a perfect solution.

Several locomotives, including Nos E5004, E5005 and E5011, had changes made to the bodyside louvres. In the case of Nos E5004 and E5011 several of the existing louvres were plated over, and those remaining were changed to vertical Krapf & Lex type ventilators and filters. These new mountings and filter frames were designed at Brighton between September and December 1960. Following overhaul at Eastleigh, No E5004 returned to traffic on 13 May 1961 with this modification.

No E5005 retained its original pattern of louvre, though as with the other two locomotives several of the lower ones were plated over. This was done as it had been found that these lower filters were sucking in brake dust and a horizontal divide was added halfway down the louvres. Both Nos E5005 and E5011 had the 'A' side louvres located either side of the central window also plated over; No E5004 was left unmodified.

Prior to this experiment some locomotives had been running in service with modified air intakes with no ducts to the main equipment. The locomotive body being used as a settling tank for dust once air had passed through the oil-wetted mesh filters of the intakes.

The first locomotive built, No E5024 (the renumbered E5000), was another locomotive to have the air intake grilles modified, though not as extensively as the work done on Nos E5004 and E5011. In this case the two grilles either side of the window on the 'A' side where the gangway through the locomotive was located were blanked over. On the 'B' side where the majority of the ventilation grilles were located, only the middle grille above the BR totem was blanked off and sheeted over. It remained in this condition until it was taken to Crewe for conversion to an electro-diesel.

Another early change was the addition in May 1961 of two brackets on the bodysides near the cab doors to hold the arrows in place for when the locomotives were used on the 'Golden Arrow' Pullman service. Another small detail change made around this time was a change in the shape of the sandbox lids from round to square. The change had been introduced during the latter stages of their construction and the earlier locomotives were modified as they passed through works.

Pioneer HA No E5024 stabled at Crewe South on 23 October 1966 whilst en route to Crewe works and conversion to an electro-diesel. The shoegear and pantograph have been removed along with the roof mounted whistle. The locomotive's revised 'B' side ventilation grille arrangement, where the central grille below the BR totem has been blanked off, is clear to see. *Class 47 Preservation Project Archive*

It was at this time that work started on designing rainstrips which ran along the roof line and onto the cab roof. Provision of this had been discussed when the locomotives were being designed but nothing certain had been agreed. This modification was first seen from 1963 onwards as the class passed through Eastleigh works, with all locomotives eventually so fitted. In all likelihood it seems that No E5020 was the first recipient when released from Eastleigh works in February 1963. No E5014 was another early recipient being seen with the strip after its overhaul at Eastleigh which was completed in April 1963. Most locomotives had either already appeared in the new unlined green livery when they acquired the rainstrips or were painted in unlined green at the same time. However No E5019 was one exception in that it ran in the original lined green colour scheme with cab rainstrips.

The circumstances of the derailment at Longfield on 10 September 1963 led to a modification to the locomotives' braking system. When the train parted between the first and second vans, although the vacuum pipes had become disconnected, there had been no automatic brake application as there should have been. This was because the conductor rail supply was short-circuited causing the locomotive's protective equipment to operate. This in turn stopped the booster from working along with the 'line' exhauster. As a result of the break in the vacuum brake pipe, the vacuum fell to zero before the 'battery' exhauster could start working. This meant that the air-vacuum valve reverted to air-braked condition meaning the locomotive's brakes did not respond to the loss of vacuum in the vacuum train pipe.

To overcome this situation, a magnet valve was added to the air-vacuum isolating valve. The magnet valve was energised when the exhauster switch was 'off', ie the air-braked condition, and de-energised when the exhauster was on, when a vacuum braked train was being worked. When de-energised it would ensure that control vacuum once created did not fall below 21in hg until vacuum working was stopped.

A comprehensive testing programme commenced in 1963, continuing into 1964, using locomotive No E5013. This work was undertaken jointly by English Electric Co Ltd and the Southern Region's own technical staff. It formed part of an intensive investigation to improve the performance of the locomotives. The class had a notoriously poor flashover record and a number of factors pointed to wheelslip being one of the primary causes. All of the locomotives had also suffered incidences of unexplained damage to the resilient gear drives. During the summer of 1964, No E5013 was used on a series of test trains from Hither Green with stock composed of former 6PUL motor cars and 4COR trailers.

The wheelslip protection system as fitted to these locomotives was fairly rudimentary and only partially effective. The impending Bournemouth electrification scheme included a requirement for 10 converted electro-diesel locomotives to be able to operate in push-pull mode. This requirement made the provision of foolproof automatic wheelslip control system an imperative requirement particularly when the driver was at the opposite end of the train. The locomotives would, when pushing, be un-manned and thus had to be totally self-protecting. The test results were detailed in a technical paper by H. W. Lucas and B. Wojtas in entitled 'Automatic Wheelslip Control' and presented to the Institution of Locomotive Engineers, London on 14 November 1966. It gave a detailed understanding of wheelslip behaviour and the electrical and mechanical consequences on this class of locomotive.

The booster locomotives were at a fundamental disadvantage when compared the AC locomotives being developed at that time for the West Coast 25kv electrification in that the AC locomotives had their motors grouped in parallel and voltage control was by transformer tap changer. The parallel connection with a (nominally) fixed voltage supply meant that a slipping motor had very little effect on any other motor. The voltage for all the motors was being held basically constant. This also applied to DC locomotives fitted with line voltage motors running in parallel grouping.

However the only practical circuit arrangement for a booster loco was for the four motors to be in two parallel pairs in series with each other and with the booster generator connected between the motor pairs. The voltage between the two motor groups was not fixed but was influenced by the voltage differences of the two motor groups at any given moment.

The consequences of this circuit arrangement are best illustrated by examining an Oscillogram record taken during an uncorrected slip during a run one by of the test trains. The test locomotive, No E5013, had been fitted with current relay control of notching as part of the test programme. This enabled the maximum tractive effort to be pre-set for each test as required. The locomotive had also been fully instrumented with recorders measuring motor voltage, current, wheel speed, and booster generator current amongst others. This enabled a detailed analysis of the effects of wheelspin to be undertaken.

The route used was the rising gradient between Hither Green and Grove Park, about 11 miles including one section at 1 in 75. The locomotive was running with the No 4 axle leading, with the train speed 44mph. At that point, motors No 4 and 3 both began slipping, apparently simultaneously.

If assuming that only one motor had started spinning, for example motor No 4, its self-generated voltage (back EMF) would increase. The voltage at its terminals would therefore rise, and being series connected with the other motor pair, motors Nos 1 and 2, there was nothing in the circuit to prevent this. As the parallel connected motor (No 3) was being subjected to this voltage rise, it is almost inevitable that that this motor would also start slipping.

During this slipping, motors Nos 4 and 3 were taking the same current, the wheelslip differential current relay did not detect anything and as a consequence did not operate. The slipping motors No 3 and 4 continued to accelerate. After about 4 seconds they reached an equivalent speed of 94mph. Their voltage was now 940 volts. The other pair of motors Nos 1 and 2 were having to share the total available voltage, this being Line Volts + Booster Generator volts (about 1,340 volts + losses). They were losing power, having only 400 volts to work with. At about 950 volts, the 750 volt motor No 4 flashed over, and was short circuited. This short circuit actually protected Motor No 3 from a flash over. However as a result of this, motors Nos 1 and 2 suddenly had the full approximately 1,350volts, double their working voltage, imposed upon them due to the short circuit on motors Nos 3 and 4. Motors Nos 1 and 2 then flashed over due to the current rising beyond their commutation limit. This flashover developed in two stages, firstly arcing between the brush boxes, then about a ¼ second later, there was arcing between the brush boxes and earth.

The brush to brush arcing imposed a short circuit through the armatures which acted as a very powerful dynamic brake force. In that ¼ second motors Nos 1 and 2 skidded and had slowed down from the train speed of 44mph to about 20mph. The

Above: **The brackets fitted to the bodysides in 1961 to carry the golden arrows when working the 'Golden Arrow' Pullman service each day.**
Jane Lilley

Below: **The locomotive used in the wheelslip trials, No E5013, in use on the Central Division working a boat train service from Victoria to Newhaven. This mid-sixties view has No E5013 heading south in the Wandsworth Common area with such a train. Interestingly, the locomotive is running without its pantograph, something which would have precluded its use on some freight duties and probably accounts for its use on this train.**
Class 47 Preservation Project Archive

Problems were encountered with the original spoked wheels and various experiments were made with solid ones. In time both types became interchangeable with locomotives using both types, sometimes on the same bogie. The preserved No E5001 has one bogie with each type. *Simon Lilley*

equivalent tractive force required to achieve this was calculated to be at least 33,000lb for each axle. This level of instantly applied reverse stress almost certainly caused damage to the gear transmission, being several times the normal maximum stress the gears would be subjected to when in service.

By this point, the locomotive's protection system had begun operating, and had shut off power. The skidding motors took another 1½ seconds to regain normal speed and the slipping pair about five seconds to slow down to the train's speed. Up to now the class had suffered from transmission troubles, mainly cracks in the gear teeth. Here then was an explanation for both this problem, and the locomotives' poor flashover record.

Considerable development and trial of control schemes continued with the aim of producing a safe and workable means of rapidly arresting wheelslip so as to limit loss of tractive effort, and then to restore power automatically up to the actual adhesion level available at that time. A requirement was that the system needed to avoid repeated slipping and large changes to tractive effort which would be especially unsafe when hauling loose coupled freight trains, at the time still a traffic requirement.

The ultimate system chosen was to use solid state control of the booster generator field. This was very fast acting and easily adjusted to maintain tractive effort around the maximum adhesion available. This system was to be fitted to the 10 locomotives converted to electro-diesels as part of the Bournemouth electrification scheme. The remaining HA electric locomotives were left unmodified.

One conclusion drawn from the tests was that they had shown that any locomotive having the power to operate very close to the adhesion limit, such as the HA class, really did require automatic wheelslip control, and not just push-pull fitted locomotives. It was no longer sensible to expect the driver to react fast enough to control wheelslip and maximise the locomotives performance at the same time.

As part of this development work, No E5013 had significant modifications made to its electrical circuits. There were modifications to the overspeed trip circuitry, with one of the two Control Camshaft Motors having been omitted. A lockout relay was provided on the overspeed trip apparatus and there were modifications, along with additional wiring and components, to the camshaft control and control camshaft position regulator circuitry.

The last modification to the class was the fitting of a small ventilator on the outer cab pillars as seen here in the picture of No 71006 at Ashford.
Class 47 Preservation Project Archive

The wiring diagrams prepared show that the booster starting position regulator was omitted and instead a booster motor polarised current relay, as well as a pantograph overload relay, were provided. The overall effect of these various changes was that current limiting control to the traction circuits was redesigned enabling, where road conditions were favourable, the 'Run Up' position to be used from rest.

The changes to the wiring diagram for this particular locomotive were completed on 27 July 1964, with the locomotive itself released back into traffic from a casual repair at Eastleigh on 13 October 1964. There was nothing externally to suggest the locomotive was any different from the others in the class and it ran in this condition until it was withdrawn.

As a result of the incident at Petts Wood in April 1964 involving No E5009, alterations to the pantograph were made and now designed to shut down automatically at 20ft 9in above rail height. An overload relay was provided to limit the current drawn from the pantograph. If the relay operated, the pantograph contactor opened and the pantograph itself lowered automatically.

One planned modification that did not happen was the change from a warning whistle to warning horns. Whilst the three Co-Co booster locomotives were modified around 1965, the HA locomotives were not. The 24 HA locomotives were included in the Southern Region's budget submission for the work which also included a large part of their electric multiple-unit fleet. Further evidence of the planned change can be found in set of Drivers Instructions from the time which indicates clearly that the change would be made from whistle to horn. Indeed the design work was even started in early 1965 on this modification, which would have cost around £59 per locomotive.

Over the course of time, solid wheels were fitted in place of the original spoked ones athough the use of spoked wheels never totally died out. The wheelsets on both the Class 71s and 74s also gave problem with loose tyres, an example being in the autumn of 1964 which saw a number of the HA locomotives out of service with loose tyres. This combined with a higher than usual number of the Southern Region's BRCW Type 3 diesel locomotives being unavailable resulted in at least six BR/Sulzer Type 2s placed on temporary loan from the London Midland Region. It also caused the brief reappearance of steam on a small number of workings.

The driver's safety device required modification. This was a problem that affected a number of different locomotive types, not just the Class HA electrics. The Works and Equipment Committee studied the problem on 25 April 1967. The existing pedal arrangements were proving unsatisfactory and would not 'fail safe' as required. The committee recommended the fitting of a new device. This would have entailed an initial spend of £200,000 up to the end of 1968.

BR Board member John Ratter produced a memorandum for the Board on the issue dated 4 May. He said that Brigadier Langley of the Railway Inspectorate had produced a specification based on that fitted in Belgian locomotives and the current equipment as fitted in both the Class HA electric locomotives and the three Southern Railway booster locomotives did not meet requirements. Mr Ratter proposed that a three-position pedal was fitted. This would have release, floating, and depressed positions. Unless the pedal remained in the middle 'floating' position and moved to 'depressed' position at least once a minute, a horn would sound and seven seconds later an emergency brake application would be applied. The same would happen if the pedal was moved to the 'release' position. Priority was to be given to locomotives used on mainline passenger services, the Class 71s clearly fitting into that category. The cost of the modifications was budgeted at £300 per locomotive.

Towards the end of 1970, the *Railway Observer* reported that Class 71 No E5013 had been fitted with push-pull equipment. The report continued by saying that trials had been run during the first two weeks of November with the locomotive and three 4CEP units throughout the South Eastern Division.

An experiment was tried with monobloc wheels on several Class 71s. The wheels used were rim sprayed which gave class 'E' properties. These wheels were seen to be satisfactory in service apart from a tendency to shelling or spooling during their first 'life'.

The experience gained from this experiment led to the development of a specification of a material called C52TS. This was expected to be less prone to thermal damage and was intended to be used on the monobloc wheels for the Class 87 AC electric locomotives then under construction at Crewe. To gain some service experience with the new material it was proposed initially to fit five Class 71s with this type of wheel. Initially at least they were fitted to Nos E5002 and E5006. By October 1973 the first results were available. In parallel a service trial (DL/265) was started of monobloc wheels made out of this material and fitted to a group of Class 47 diesel locomotives allocated to the Eastern and Western Regions. This was to assess their suitability as a replacement for 'D'-type tyred wheels then in use which were prone to loose tyres.

Comparisons of tyre wear between the locomotives on the three regions were not easy as the method of reporting flange wear was not uniform. Two different methods were used and these did not produce uniform data. A further complication was that of the two Class 71 locomotives; No E5002 had its wheels turned for tyre flats after 25,000 miles and measurements of the wheels before turning were not taken. Furthermore, it could not be guaranteed that the wheels had been turned to a true P1 profile. The only comparison that could be made was on the basis of wear rate.

Both locomotives were initially fitted with wheels made from the C52TS material. Examination of both locomotives was undertaken after they had run around 52,000 miles in service with the new type of wheels. The number two wheelset of the number one bogie from No E5006 had needed to be removed having run 15,000 miles as it was found that the left-hand wheel was wearing at an abnormal rate. On closer examination damage on the wheel was found to be a regular pattern of polished zones, along with fine cracking all over the tread. The tread condition was good, apart from some mild cracking and slight spalling. In comparison the condition of the conventional 'D' tyred wheelset which replaced the one removed at 15,000 miles was noticeably worse, despite the lower mileage. Cracking, although moderate, was worse than that on the C52TS wheels apart from one. Comparisons were also made with wear on 'D' tyres fitted to Class 74 locomotives. The wheelsets on No E5002 gave similar results according to the report.

Delays in starting the experiment meant that the original objective of providing data on this type of wheel in readiness for their use on the Class 87 AC electric locomotives was missed. However, the October 1973 report recommended that the experiment was continued. This would maximise the available data on the relative performance of class 'D' tyres and C52TS wheels. It would also confirm or indeed deny the assumption that data gathered from one type of locomotive could provide a practical guide to behaviour on another class. In future, locomotives would be fitted with only one experimental bogie.

A further report was produced in March 1974. The fitting of locomotives with C52TS wheels had been suspended following the discovery of excessive wear on one wheel (No E5006). The cause was found to be incorrect heat treatment. At the time of this second report, March 1974, it was planned to fit one bogie of several more Class 71s with the C52TS wheels. This second report also made more direct comparisons between experiment DL/265 on the Class 47s, and experiment EL/36 on the Class 71s. Three Class 71s were part of the experiment at this time: Nos 71002 and 71006 with the C52TS wheels, with No 71003 used as the comparison locomotive with the 'D' type tyres. Tread damage was found to be light.

A very late modification, applied to all fourteen locomotives, was the fitting of an additional cab ventilator. These were fitted to the outer windscreen pillars of the cabs.

7
The HB Electro-Diesels
Origins

Above: **JA type electro-diesel No E6003 stabled at Eastleigh. The six JA electro-diesels were trialled extensively and proved the worth and capability of the dual-powered concept. It meant that the straight electric HA type locomotives appeared less flexible by comparison.**
Class 47 Preservation Project Archive

As Phase Two of the Kent Coast Electrification Scheme was completed, so thoughts turned to other schemes. The Southern Area Board considered a memorandum from the General Manager C. P. Hopkins on 5 July 1962, looking at proposals for the further electrification of certain lines on both the South Western and Central Divisions. Such extensions would use the existing third-rail 750v DC system and would be schemes where management could be sure that both early and satisfactory financial returns could be obtained. Of some interest is the fact that the memorandum said that high-powered motor coaches would be used in push-pull formation on high speed trains; the basis of course for the Bournemouth electrification.

Within weeks of this first discussion, a draft proposal for extending electric traction to Bournemouth was circulated by Mr Hopkins. Dated 14 August, it envisaged the need for 21 3,000hp/600hp electro-diesel locomotives with the class calculated to run 793,000 miles between them per year. This initial requirement was however modified very quickly. A second proposal, dated 5 September, saw the number of locomotives reduced by one, but with their annual mileage increased to 1,031,000. Of the twenty locomotives, 17 would be in use and three would be standing spare at any given time. This scheme also identified a need for 45 1,600hp electro-diesel locomotives.

This revised scheme was discussed by the Southern Region's Traction Committee on 12 September. They agreed that the Southern Area Board should have the opportunity to examine the proposals in detail at a special meeting to be held on 20 September prior to the scheme's submission to the BTC. The Commission's Chief Electrical Engineer (CEE) S. B. Warder indicated that that he was ready to submit the Bournemouth scheme to the Chief Inspecting Officer at the Ministry of Transport Brigadier Langley for his approval.

The Southern Area Board met on 20 September and after a long discussion of the proposals, agreed to the Bournemouth electrification scheme being submitted to the BTC for consideration. The proposal C. P. Hopkins put forwards to the BTC on 8 October, contained a requirement for 20 3,000hp/600hp electro-diesel locomotives.

The 'Plastic' Locomotive

The Southern Region's initial thoughts on a Bournemouth scheme electro-diesel centred on a locomotive having an electric power one-hour rating of 3,000hp. Such a locomotive, had it come to fruition, may well have made extensive use of GRP in its construction according to surviving BR documents from the time. To this end, R. G. Jarvis and his design team at Brighton had been working in conjunction with the renowned industrial designer Frederick Ashford on such a concept. A study of the Brighton Drawing Register indicates that the first work started around 19 September 1962. There was no further work though until 2 January 1963, when a proposed cab profile drawing was produced. This was followed on 25 January by one of the proposed air intakes.

In March 1963, Mr Ashford was able to submit proposals to BR's Principal Design Officer George Williams. These consisted of layouts and coloured perspectives based on drawings supplied by the drawing office at Brighton.

On 13 May 1963, a meeting was held at Brighton to discuss future locomotive and rolling stock projects. On the agenda was the possible use of Glass Reinforced Plastic (GRP) as a material for use in locomotive construction. The 3,000hp locomotive was one project discussed at length with a view to using GRP for much of the bodywork.

For this meeting, Mr Ashford produced a model of a possible locomotive showing two different design options (regretfully no image of this model appears to have survived). In the discussion that followed a number of design issues were debated. Given the electro-diesel concept was one specifically for the Southern Region, the question was should it be treated as a styling 'one-off' or resemble other recent BR locomotives such as the Brush Type 4?

The design envisaged that much of the lighter equipment including the engine cooling unit, air inlets, and air filters would be in roof mounted and removable GRP moulded units. These would extend downwards to form the bodyside as far as waist level.

The meeting agreed that no definite progress could be made on the new locomotive's mechanical design until a prototype had been authorised. At that point a development order could then be placed with English Electric Co Ltd for the electrical equipment. Until further information was available on that aspect from English Electric Co Ltd there was little further design work that could be accomplished at Brighton. Indeed, little further design work was undertaken by BR, although on 3 February 1964, two drawings were produced, both providing a diagram and data for a 3,000/650hp electro-diesel. The only difference between the two was one had a wheel diameter of 3ft 7in, the other a wheel diameter of 3ft 9in.

An early indication however that BR's thinking might be moving away from the 3,000/600hp concept came in April 1964. That month's edition of *Railway Magazine* reported that the Southern Region had now devised an electric push-pull locomotive 78 tons in weight and rated at 2,500hp.

Mr Ashford continued with his work though, to the point where when he met R. G. Jarvis in May he was able to provide a model of a potential 3,000hp/600hp electro-diesel locomotive. Clearly though Jarvis' thinking was different. In a letter to George Williams, BR's Director of Industrial Design,

HA electric locomotive No E5005 stands outside Crewe works in March 1967. It has for company an English Electric Type 4, a recently overhauled Brush Type 4, and an AL6 AC electric locomotive. *Class 47 Preservation Project Archive*

on 28 May he said 'you will appreciate that when the locomotive is ultimately designed, we shall doubtless follow more closely the cab form of the Brush Type 4'. At this stage the locomotive was still very much a concept, no authorisation had been sought or indeed been given to take the project forwards to the point of building of a locomotive.

Indeed, no further progress was made in the weeks that followed, which prompted Mr Ashford to write to George Williams on 15 June to enquire about progress. In his reply Williams said that he had been advised by Mr Jarvis that no authority had yet been given for these locomotives. He went on to assure Ashford that when the time came he would be the design consultant appointed to the project.

BR's Industrial Design Department's 'Work in Hand Report' published on 17 September said that work on this project was at a standstill. Whilst preliminary drawings and a model had been completed in the autumn of 1963 for a new bodyshell design and cab interior work was in abeyance pending a decision on the construction method, most probably using GRP.

In the aftermath of the announcement of the Bournemouth scheme, Frederick Ashford wrote again to George Williams on 7 October to ask again about progress. Two days later Williams had an update on the project from Jarvis. The 3,000hp/600hp locomotive was now in abeyance Jarvis advised, and an exercise was now underway to determine whether it was both feasible and economically sound to convert the 2,500hp Bo-Bo electric locomotives to electro-diesels.

On 23 October 1964, Mr Jarvis wrote to George Williams again on the subject. In his letter he said that it was 'now practically decided that the 3,000/600hp electro-diesel will not be built and the existing 2,500hp electric locomotives will be converted'. He continued, 'to justify this, the cost is to be kept to a minimum and it is proposed to retain the existing underframes, cabs, and bogies. New bodysides and roof will be fitted'. Jarvis concluded by saying that he would be consulting with Williams when they were in a position to determine where the bodyside air inlets and windows were to be positioned.

Developments Elsewhere

Whilst work was continuing on what the larger electro-diesel might look like and indeed be made out of, the Southern Region was continuing to refine its proposals for the Bournemouth electrification. A paper on the scheme dated 21 August 1963 saw a further revision of the locomotive requirements. In this proposal, 18 3,000/600hp electro-diesel locomotives would be required. This would see 15 locomotives in use at any given time, with the remainder undergoing maintenance. A need was also specified for 40 of the 1,600/600hp electro-diesels. Twelve of these would be sent to the Central and South Eastern Divisions to enable the release of 19 BRCW Type 3 locomotives that would be needed for the push-pull passenger service between Bournemouth and Weymouth.

BR's CEE SB Warder in his periodic report to the BR Board dated 12 December 1963 said that consideration had been given to the design of more powerful electrical equipment that would be required for the Bournemouth scheme if it were given the go-ahead. If the 3,000/600hp electro-diesel locomotive was to be realised, there was the need for the production of prototype equipment, and he recommended that such an order be placed with English Electric Co Ltd.

A further document dated 31 January 1964 entitled 'Report on the Extension of Electric and Diesel-Electric Traction on the South Western Division' was prepared by the General Manager's office. This reduced the requirement for 3,000/600hp electro-diesel locomotives down to 10. This figure had been achieved by what was described as 'ruthless pruning'. The annual mileage was estimated at 91,000 miles per locomotive

This report was further refined and the Southern Region agreed its proposals for the Bournemouth scheme in a document dated 14 May 1964. Here, the 10 3,000/600hp electro-diesel locomotives specified would all be in use at any given time. Type 3 diesel locomotives would be used in their place on the most suitable diagrams when one of these electro-diesel locomotives was unavailable. The planned annual mileage was still 912,000 for the whole class; of that total 867,000 would be on electric power, with the remaining 45,000 on diesel power.

The scheme then made its way through the long-established approval processes; the Works & Equipment Committee accepted the scheme on 2 June, with BR's Planning Committee discussing the proposals on 17 June. The BR Board approved the Bournemouth scheme on 25 June 1964. Ministerial approval was granted on 21 September, one of the final acts of the Conservative Government before the General Election on 15 October.

Following Warder's report to the BR Board in December 1963, a limited development contract worth £5,000 was placed with English Electric Co Ltd for the electrical equipment required for a 3,000/600hp electro-diesel locomotive. Preliminary work was also underway within BR. The CME J. F. Harrison estimated the new locomotives' cost to be £950,000 with a further £50,000 required to cover the various development expenses. There was, he said in a memorandum to the Planning Committee co-authored with S. B. Warder the CEE and L. W. Ibbotson the Chief Operating Officer, 'a prima facie case for continuing with the development work'. There were three main reasons for a having a locomotive of this type. Firstly it was to ensure uniform performance with the planned EMU stock for the Bournemouth scheme. Secondly it was more economical to use a locomotive of this type, than either Type 4 diesel locomotives or more 1,600/600hp electro-diesels. Finally by avoiding double-heading with the smaller electro-diesel type, there would be no need to restrict train lengths or undertake major civil engineering work at Waterloo to lengthen platforms.

Whilst there was a clear need for a larger electro-diesel, the means by which that would be achieved was now becoming the subject of intense debate and discussion. When the Bournemouth Electrification Project Committee met on 8 October, the proposal to convert a number of HA electric locomotives rather than build new locomotives was described as 'now being pursued actively'. A meeting had been held already to examine its technical feasibility. Mr Hoff of BR's Supplies Department was asked to contact English Electric Co Ltd to see if they had the capacity to produce the equipment for the 3,000/600hp locomotives, were that option to be chosen.

Further evidence of the conversion option being pursued actively came at the Southern Region Management meeting on 19 October. Whilst a converted 2,500hp locomotive would not give exactly the same performance as a 3,000hp locomotive, such a locomotive might well be acceptable to meet requirements. When the same group met eight days later they were told that an early decision on locomotives for the Bournemouth scheme was needed.

Three days later on 22 October, a meeting was held at Brighton to discuss the merits of both the 3,000hp new build and 2,500hp conversion options. Representatives from all the interested departments were present, BR's CEE, Mechanical Engineer (Design), CM&EE Southern Region, General Manager Southern Region, and Workshops Eastleigh. The key issues were discussed at length including physical layout, overall weight, electrical equipment, auxiliary power, costs, design programme, and a range of other factors such as shoegear and push-pull equipment.

Regardless of the option chosen, the key decision had to be made on how the diesel engine would be attached to the booster equipment. Two possible options were available, one involving mechanical drive using an Orthlinghaus clutch, the other via a generator. There were advantages and disadvantages to both. The mechanical drive option was seen as a novel approach using a clutch previously untried in a traction application. A special control system would be needed to adjust the engine and booster speeds prior to engagement, for the proposed Orthlinghaus clutch, and the relative speeds could not exceed 600rpm. Concerns were raised about the possible torsional stresses on the diesel engine. Lastly, there was a possible maintenance issue in that there was a risk of misalignment with unit replacement.

The other option to fit a generator to the diesel engine presented far fewer technical problems but meant an increase of the locomotives' weight and a greater cost. The larger size of the generator option meant that if conversion was chosen, some of the equipment cabinets would need to be reconstructed or repositioned. It was agreed that this and a number of other technical issues needed further investigation and that these should be examined urgently. The results of these various technical investigations would enable a final decision to be made in around three months' time.

The outcome of the meeting was that conversion instead of new build was now the preferred way forwards, and that the SR's CM&EE should put forward this option to David McKenna the General Manager.

S. B. Warder updated the BR Board on the various issues being considered on 1 November. He told them that a recent review had shown that 2,500hp being available for electric operation of the locomotives was in fact adequate. The conversion proposal had been discussed by himself, the CME J. F. Harrison, the Southern Region CM&EE W. J. A. Sykes, and representatives from English Electric Co Ltd. A decision to convert locomotives rather than build new ones had been agreed on the grounds of economy and operating advantage.

The next day was the latest Southern Region Management meeting. It heard that another 23 locomotives were needed for the Bournemouth scheme. Ten of these would be either new 3,000/600hp locomotives or 2,500/600hp converted ones. Conversion was seen as the better option. It was scheduled to withdraw the 10 HA locomotives from February 1966 onwards to enable the conversion work to be carried out. The withdrawal of the requisite locomotives however could not take place until there were sufficient numbers of 1,600/600hp electro-diesel locomotives available to replace them. Meanwhile, discussion on the technical issues surrounding both the new build and conversion options was continuing between BR Headquarters and the Southern Region.

W. J. Sykes wrote to David McKenna setting out in great detail the case for converting rather than building 10 new locomotives on 16 November 1964. He wrote that after discussions with both J. F. Harrison and S. B. Warder it had been agreed that conversion was technically feasible, though some details remained to be resolved. That work though should be complete within a matter of weeks.

The case for conversion rather than building new locomotives, centred on two main considerations. Firstly, there was a cost saving in converting 10 HA electric locomotives plus building 10 additional 1,600/600hp electro-diesel locomotives to replace those being converted. This he estimated at around £21,000 per locomotive. The cost of the conversion work itself was put at roughly £30,000 per locomotive.

The second and indeed the key factor in opting for conversion over new build, was the time taken to produce the new locomotives. With the new build option, it could take between six and nine months before the electrical equipment was developed sufficiently to allow the detailed mechanical design work to be done. That work would take between 18 and 24 months. Even if construction could be completed within a year, it is unlikely the locomotives would be available before the end of 1967.

Were the conversion option to be chosen, it would be possible to finalise the electrical design within three months. Drawings for the mechanical conversion would be completed within a year, meaning the design work overall would be completed by early 1966. At this point 13 1,600/600hp locomotives would start to be available for traffic, so allowing the 10 HA locomotives to be withdrawn for conversion. He said that provision of 10 2,500/600hp electro-diesel locomotives by June 1967 was perfectly possible. In concluding, he recommended adopting the conversion option, and that the development work on the 3,000hp locomotive should be stopped.

Mr McKenna was not long in making up his mind on the issue, giving his approval for the conversion option on 25 November.

No E6106 at Clapham. The rebuilding work required a new bodyshell to be constructed. On the A side only two ventilation grilles and a window were required.
Class 47 Preservation Project Archive

Conversion Work Begins

The provision of the locomotives and rolling stock for the Bournemouth scheme was monitored by the monthly meetings of the Rolling Stock Group. The group's members included representatives from the Southern Region General Manager's and CM&EE's departments, BR's Workshop Division, and the BR CME department. The meeting minutes, like those of the Electrification Committee for the Kent Coast schemes before it, tells us step by step what was happening and when as these various issues and delays arose and were dealt with. There were a number of other committees and groups meeting which had an interest in the scheme's progress and when all of these are taken together they give a clear picture of the conversion of the HA electric locomotives into the HB electro-diesels.

The Rolling Stock Group's first meeting was held on 7 January 1965. The Southern Region confirmed that the larger electro-diesels would be required for the start of electric services in March 1967. The power transmission issue was still to be resolved and this was a matter that should be resolved early on in the project. The speed at which the design work could be completed depended on an early decision being made. The design office advised the region that provided the decision was made by 22 January the design work could be completed by early 1966. When the Project Committee met on 11 February, they were told that the generator option had been chosen and that design work could proceed. The Drawing Register shows that design work for converting HA locomotives to electro-diesel configuration began at Brighton on 23 February 1965.

The initial locomotive conversion programme prepared on 19 February envisaged the locomotives being in works for a total of 20 weeks. Work would start in January 1966 and continue until completion in January 1967.

By the time the Rolling Stock Group met on 3 March, Workshop Production Charts had been produced setting out the basic timescales for the conversion work. The Workshops Division was asked to review these timescales and advise if they could be met. Most of the locomotive specification had been handed over to the Brighton Drawing Office, with only the one for the brake gear still outstanding. The meeting also discussed the question of locomotive tyres. There had been some problems with those fitted on the HA locomotives and the view was that any changes should be made as part of the conversion work.

Authority for the conversion work was given by the BR Board on 10 June, as a variation to the Bournemouth scheme. The overall cost of the work was estimated at £425,000 as compared to the £935,000 budgeted originally for building new locomotives. A few weeks later on 29 June, authority was sought and obtained from the Supply Committee for the purchase of the electrical equipment from English Electric at a cost of £203,000.

The conversion work on the 10 locomotives encountered a number of delays. The reasons for these being many and varied; and indeed from very early on problems were encountered. Authorisation for BR Workshops to carry out the conversion work was granted by the Supply Committee on 2 September. The price for the work was to be finalised when the design work had been completed. The first set of electrical equipment was scheduled to be delivered by English Electric in December 1966, with one set per month after that until September 1967. Discussions were planned with English Electric to see if this could be improved upon. BR Workshops were saying that they could deliver the first locomotive in March 1967 with one locomotive a month after that, with deliveries completed in December 1967.

Discussions with English Electric took place soon after with the result that that H. R. Gomersal who was BR's Chief Officer (New Works) was able to advise the Works & Equipment and Supply Committees that a revised delivery scheduled had been agreed. The new schedule would enable Crewe to deliver three converted locomotives by March 1967 with subsequent deliveries at a rate of one per month.

As the New Year came around, there was no change in the planned delivery dates of the converted locomotives. Indeed in a report to the BR Board on 18 February 1966 it was understood that just three locomotives would be available for the start of electric services in 1967. In addition, the first locomotive for conversion No E5015 had arrived at Crewe. In advance of it being taken north, the bogie mounted shoegear was removed along with the roof mounted pantograph and the cab whistle. On 30 January it was parked in the arrival sidings at the works. By 27 February the locomotive itself was nowhere to be seen, apart from its cabs which were stored in the Erecting shop.

The early optimism on delivery dates did not last very long. The Rolling Stock Group minutes from 9 March record that some delays had been encountered in the design work due to a shortage of design staff at Brighton. By the following meeting on 6 April, vital drawings had been delayed and that as such the programme would have to be pushed back a month although it was hoped that this time could be made up later on. Efforts were made to obtain additional design staff to ease the problem but without success. It was now expected that the first locomotive would be completed at the end of February 1967 and already some four to six weeks later than previously planned.

By April two locomotives were at Crewe for conversion, No E5016 was seen in the Erecting shop being made ready for conversion on 24 April. The decision as to which locomotives were selected is not defined although this may simply have been based on those which came due for overhaul.

A meeting between the CE (T&RS), BR Workshops, and English Electric was held at Crewe on 11 May. The aim was to establish the up-to-date position regarding locomotive deliveries. The outcome was a revised delivery programme which confirmed the first locomotive being ready at the end of February 1967, with deliveries being made at the rate of one per month after that. The final locomotive would arrive in November 1967. It had been planned to start electric running but on the existing steam timings in March 1967, with the full electric timetable being introduced on 12 June, but as things stood only four of the new locomotives would likely be available for service by then. At a further meeting between all the parties held at English Electric's Preston works on 2 June, it was agreed that a revised programme would be prepared by all concerned.

June saw another locomotive, No E5006, in transit to Crewe.

An internal memorandum on the situation dated 20 June aimed to identify some of the causes of the likely late delivery of locomotives. The main reason given was the decision to opt for converting locomotives rather than building new and the consequent delay in placing equipment orders. The lateness of the decision meant that English Electric were unable to quote a delivery date for equipment earlier than December 1966. Also the extent of the work required to convert the locomotives had not been made clear at the time. The memorandum said that it had been necessary to reduce the main superstructure back to the main longitudinal sections and to commence the rebuild from there.

Locomotives continued to be taken to Crewe for conversion despite the delays being experienced. By early July, three locomotives were there and progress was being made on producing the remaining designs at Brighton. Some drawings were still outstanding and a meeting was held on 8 July to review progress. Subject to these outstanding drawings being produced, it was thought the first locomotive would be ready by February 1967.

By the middle of the month the situation had changed. The Works & Equipment Committee at their meeting held on 19 July heard that delivery of the control gear from English Electric would be delayed by a month. The reason given was the heavy concentration of work for BR, with priority being given to equipment for Bournemouth scheme's EMU stock. As a result, the first locomotive was not now expected to be completed until the end of March 1967.

The Rolling Stock Group met on 10 August. There were now three locomotives at Crewe with a fourth expected to be sent north in October. Design progress was described as difficult, but there was co-operation from Crewe works and it was expected that requirements would be met. However, the news from English Electric was that the control equipment was not now expected to be ready until February 1967. The effect of this meant that delivery of the first locomotive would be delayed until May 1967 and that none of the 10 locomotives would be available for traffic by June. The Southern Region would have to plan for operating during part of the winter of 1967 at least, without all 10 locomotives having been delivered. Concern was also expressed by the Workshops Division representative at the meeting, Mr C. R. Allman, that Crewe may have to break the production programme as a result of these equipment delays from English Electric.

As a result of the worsening delivery situation, BR, the Workshops Division, the Southern Region, and English Electric met in London on 15 August. Among the BR officials present were A. E. Robson Assistant General Manager (Production) Workshops Division, and W. J. Sykes the Southern Region's CM&EE.

The aim of the meeting was to discover the extent of the equipment delays as these had so far not been fully disclosed by English Electric. After the meeting in June a revised delivery programme had been prepared. Now just 10 weeks later the whole programme was in doubt. Mr Robson referred to the June meeting, saying he had made a specific point of ensuring that everyone was fully aware of what the requirements were.

The various contracts for the Bournemouth scheme were then reviewed in detail. English Electric admitted that the equipment for the 2,500hp electro-diesels would be delayed two months. The reasons for the delay they said were still being investigated, but the dates they had offered in June had been given in good faith and had been based on estimates from their sub-contractors. When they became aware of shortages of certain parts their investigations had shown that the commitments given by their suppliers were inadequate.

As a result of these latest delays, the first locomotive would not be delivered until May 1967. Mr Sykes said that the region had been planning the rundown of the steam locomotive fleet based on electric services starting in June 1967. They would in consequence be faced with a motive power shortage whether or not electric running started in

June. It was up to English Electric to recover the situation. The company was also told, most forcibly, that the dates they were now quoting were far outside their contractual commitments and that the BR Board reserved the right to take whatever action it needed to safeguard their position. A further meeting would be required to agree a revised programme and delivery dates and also to determine to what extent any lost time could be recovered.

A revised programme was devised following the meetings between the three parties. The view in mid-September 1966 was that completion of the first locomotive could be achieved by April 1967 rather than May as thought previously. To assist English Electric's Preston works, Crewe were used to provide help in the modification of some of the control frames.

In the meantime, work had been done by the Workshops Division on the cost of the physical work needed to convert the 10 locomotives. On 24 August they were able to say they would be able to do the work for £30,000 per locomotive.

The Rolling Stock Group's next meeting was held on 15 September. Three locomotives were at Crewe and the fourth was planned to be delivered there on 8 October. Design drawing production was still continuing down at Brighton, but was running to plan. Crewe would still be taking delivery of locomotives from the Southern Region and using the time before the control gear arrived from English Electric to progress as much of the other conversion work as possible. The locomotive delivery schedule was still that the first locomotive would be delivered at the end of April with one per month thereafter.

A report to the Works & Equipment Committee dated 21 September indicated an improvement in the delivery time of equipment from English Electric of four weeks. Even so it was unlikely that any locomotives would be ready for the start of the new electric timetable planned to operate from mid-June 1967.

The design aspect of the conversion work was causing some of the delays to the project. At a meeting held on 6 October it was learned that the whole design programme was behind schedule. This was a major issue as the production of drawings was controlling further work on the locomotives by then at Crewe and the Rolling Stock Group were given the bad news on 13 October that work at Crewe had almost stopped. This meant that deliveries of the early locomotives would undoubtedly be delayed and revised delivery programme would have to be prepared. It also meant that the return of the on loan Brush Type 4s from Cardiff would have to be re-phased.

The fourth locomotive for conversion, No E5024, was noted at Crewe South on 23 October.

Additional design resources were sought, but by the time of the next Rolling Stock Group meeting on 10 November, none had been located. However, Brighton had rescheduled their output and the design work was planned to be complete by the end of the year. The effect on production because of these delays was still being evaluated. The delivery to Crewe of locomotives for conversion was running to schedule, with the planned four locomotives now there. A further meeting was scheduled with English Electric to be held at Crewe where they would be putting forwards their equipment delivery schedule. It would be possible after that to prepare a revised locomotive delivery programme in time for the next Rolling Stock Group meeting.

By 20 November the erstwhile No E5015 was in the Erecting shop at Crewe having had its frame modified and the bodyshell structure built. In the Fabrication shop No E5016 had undergone the frame modifications and No E5024 was in the process of being modified. No E5006 was also present and was being prepared for having the frame modified.

Whilst the conversion work was progressing, BR was looking towards the time when the locomotives were in service. On 6 December the Works & Equipment Committee was asked to approve the purchase of £33,000 worth of spare parts for the new locomotives. A further £55,000 of spare parts would be reallocated from the existing HA locomotive holdings.

That meeting was held on 14 December and there was both good and bad news. The good news was that there were now five locomotives at Crewe for conversion and work on them was proceeding. The bad news was that work had been limited by electrical equipment shortages and as yet there was no firm delivery schedule from English Electric.

The following day the British Railways Board was given a progress report by the CE (T&RS). The conversion work was described as a virtual rebuild echoing sentiments expressed some months earlier. However, advantage was being taken of this to fit an advanced type of control gear which would minimise maintenance. The first locomotive was not expected to be completed until June 1967 and it was hoped to have five of the locomotives in service before the winter of 1967.

The first two locomotives Nos E5015 and E5016 were now both in the Erecting shop. The frame modifications had been completed and their new bodyshells in place. In the Fabrication shop, the next three locomotives were undergoing frame modifications. In the case of No E6103 the bodyshell work was also well advanced. The frames had been cut on No E6104 and No E6105 (formerly No E5019) was being prepared for the start of the frame work.

At this time the timescales for deliveries seemed to be changing almost daily. The Works & Equipment Committee was advised on 19 December that the conversion work had been delayed by another four weeks and as a result only four locomotives would be ex-works by October 1967. As a result of the delays the Southern Region were borrowing Brush Type 4s. However as these were not fitted with ETH they could not be used in winter. On the document is a hand written note suggesting that ETH fitted ones from the Eastern Region could be used.

Initially, there was conflicting information in the railway press as to which locomotives were earmarked for conversion. Initial reports in January 1967 said that No E5001 had been in Eastleigh works since 1 November 1966 for conversion to an electro-diesel locomotive and that another class member was at Crewe for the same purpose.

The first Rolling Stock Group meeting of 1967 was held on 19 January. By this point there were six locomotives at Crewe. A meeting had been held with English Electric on 5 January and a programme for the delivery of the control frames agreed. The first of these was scheduled to arrive at Crewe during the week ending 20 May, and the last during the week ending 10 November. English Electric was being pressed to deliver the first of the control frames by 1 April. If this date could be met, it would mean the first locomotive could be completed before the works holiday due for the first two weeks of July. Also the first four locomotives would be in the Erecting shop at Crewe by next weekend (21/22 January). Indeed, on 22 January the first four locomotives were present whilst in the Fabrication shop work was complete on modifying the frame of No E5019, whilst No E5023 was being prepared for the work.

Locomotives continued to be delivered to Crewe for conversion; seven were at Crewe by the middle of February. The eighth locomotive would be withdrawn at the end of the month and the ninth at the end of March. There was still no word from English Electric on whether they would be able to deliver the first control frame and there were continuing problems with modifications to drawings being supplied from Brighton which needed to be resolved.

By mid-March eight locomotives were at Crewe, with the other two to be delivered shortly. Whilst progress was being made the arrival at Crewe of new drawings and amendments to ones already received was causing problems. Given these problems and the ongoing problems with equipment from English Electric, it was now realised that the first locomotive would not be completed before the works holiday in July.

A visitor to Crewe on 19 March noted Nos E5006, E5015, E5016, E5023 and E5024. Three of the locomotives, had new numbers chalked on them, No E5015 to become No E6101, No E5016 to become No E6102, and No E5024 to become No E6104. Of those locomotives, No E6101 was said to be almost complete, No E6102 was now partially equipped and the bodyshell work had been completed on Nos E6103–E6106. In the Fabrication shop No E5003 had undergone the frame modifications and No E5005 was being made ready for this work to be done.

The April meeting of the Rolling Stock Group took place on the 12th. As per the program there were nine of the ten locomotives at Crewe for conversion. To resolve the ongoing issues with drawings from Brighton and changes to them, arrangements had been made for a draughtsman from Brighton to be based at Crewe two or three days a week. The meeting was also given a further revised locomotive delivery programme. The first was due for completion by 12 August and the last on 24 February 1968. This was a six week slip for the completion of the first locomotive, but a six week improvement for the delivery of the last compared to the schedule the meeting were given in March.

A meeting had been arranged with English Electric for 26 April to try to iron out any outstanding issues and with the news that one and possibly two sets of equipment were due to arrive from them by 25 April. The meeting with English Electric was later described as satisfactory. At a subsequent meeting, English Electric said the first control cubicle would not be delivered until mid-July, though this was then revised to 30 June.

By May, the conversion work on all 10 HAs was in progress. One of the Drawing Office staff from Brighton was still on site at Crewe to help with drawings. As a consequence of the cubicle delays, the locomotive delivery programme was revised once more. The first locomotive would be completed by week ending 9 September, with the final locomotive scheduled for delivery by week ending 17 February 1968. Compared to the schedule prepared in March this represented a 10 week slip. Whilst the delays with the control cubicles were the major problem, there were 35 other main parts on order from English Electric that were causing concern. If these were also delayed, then the locomotive delivery schedule would slip even further behind.

At Crewe, locomotives Nos E6101, E6102 and E6105 had been at least partially equipped. The bodyshell work had been completed on Nos E6103, E6104, E6106 and E6107 and all seven locomotives were in the Erecting shop. In the Fabrication shop, No E5017 had undergone the frame modifications, whilst No E5021 was being prepared for the work. In the Fabrications shop yard was the completed bodyshell of No E6108.

The delays being encountered with the conversion of the 10 locomotives was discussed by the Southern Region Board on 1 June. It was clear that none would be available by the start of the train heating season on 1 October and the meeting resolved to request the BRB for the loan of three more Type 4 diesels.

A further meeting was held at Crewe between BR and English Electric on 13 June. It was reported afterwards that some of the delivery difficulties had been overcome and that the delivery date of the week ending 9 September for the first converted locomotive still held good. The supply of control cubicles though remained critical.

The following day the Rolling Stock Group met, and was given an update on the meeting with English Electric. They were also advised that the first bogie would be wheeled during the week ending 24 June. Also discussed was the provision of main spares. Around 60% of general spares for the locomotives were now available, and the provision of the main spare parts still needed was being worked on.

A further visit to Crewe on 27 August showed that the former No E5015 numbered No E6101 had been painted in its new BR blue with full yellow front livery. It was now back in the Erecting shop. Also there was No E6102 which was reported to be nearing completion. Locomotives Nos E6103 to E6105 had by now been fitted with their traction equipment whilst Nos E6106 to E6109 were still just bodyshells at this point. The final locomotive No E6110 was still in the fabrication shop with the bodyshell work in progress.

Completion of the first locomotive was reported to the Works & Equipment Committee on 16 September. However tests carried out on the No E6101 prior to delivery had needed to be delayed because of defective components from English Electric. They were sending staff to Crewe to rectify the faults. As a result the first locomotive was not due to be released from Crewe until the week ending 30 September.

The HB Electro-Diesels – Origins

HA Type to HB Type Conversions

HA Type No	HB Type No	Date to Crewe	Date Released
E5015	E6101	Jan 1966	11/02/1968
E5016	E6102	April 1966	05/11/1967
E5006	E6103	June 1966	10/12/1967
E5024	E6104	Oct 1966	25/02/1968
E5019	E6105	Oct 1966	10/03/1968
E5023	E6106	Jan 1967	17/03/1968
E5003	E6107	Feb 1967	31/03/1968
E5005	E6108	March 1967	07/04/1968
E5017	E6109	April 1967	28/04/1968
E5021	E6110	May 1967	09/06/1968

The Conversion Work

The Locomotive Body and Underframe

The original body was non-load bearing carried on a stiff box-type underframe. Whilst the existing cabs were retained, a new load-bearing body was made. This was a Warren girder type structure, linked rigidly to the underframe rather than the flexible arrangement on the original locomotives. The roof was modified with the provision of removable panels, some of which were made from translucent glass reinforced plastic. One point of interest is that as part of the conversion work, the cab rain strips put on from 1963 onwards were removed and not replaced. Also removed was the roof mounted warning whistle, Trico horns, one G Flat and one E Flat, were provided in their place.

The cab interiors were largely unaltered. The main changes being associated with the revised control system and those associated with push-pull operation. This included driver-to-guard 'Loudaphone' equipment and starting bells.

Underneath the locomotive was a 310-gallon fuel tank. The only fuel gauge provided was located on the outside of the tank, meaning train crews needed to be vigilant to avoid running out of 'juice'.

A new builder's plate was made for the converted locomotives. It was an oval plate brass/chromed 10½in by 6in which read 'Rebuilt by BR Crewe 1967 POWER EQUIPMENT BY ENGLISH ELECTRIC COMPANY LIMITED'.

Bogies

The original bogies were retained but with modifications given the increased weight of the locomotive. The secondary laminated spring suspension was removed and replaced with coil springs for better control. The original shoe gear was also changed to air-operated fully retractable equipment, located between the bogie bolsters. This was necessary when working on diesel power on un-electrified lines where there could be obstructions fouling the electrification gauge. Furthermore, the original design had provided insufficient electrical clearance at times when the shoe became fouled with contaminants such as brake shoe dust or conductor rail de-icing fluid.

Due to the internal equipment layout, the axle weights differed between the two ends of the locomotive, the No 1 end weight was 21t 3cwt with the No 2 end slightly heavier at 21t 5cwt.

The Paxman Engine

The engine chosen for the HB electro-diesels was the six-cylinder Paxman 6YJXL which developed 650hp at 1,500rpm. British Railways already had traction experience with this engine, as it had been used in the Swindon built Type 1 0-6-0 diesel-hydraulic locomotives that were introduced in 1964. It had been hoped to use the English Electric four-cylinder 600hp engines as used in the JA electro-diesels, but axle-loading considerations meant this was not possible.

This was the smallest engine in Paxman's range of YJXL engines. The six cylinders were in a cast iron block in a 60o 'V' shape. The cylinder bore was 197mm with a 216mm stroke. Aluminium alloy was used for the pistons and these were oil-cooled using jets directed from the drillings in the fork and blade connecting rods. The blade connecting rods were used to drive a forged steel crankshaft which used shell inserts. The cylinder firing order was A1 B2 A3 B1 A2 B3. A Napier HP 100/INT turbo-charger was fitted.

The engines for HB locomotives were essentially the same as those for the Swindon Type 1 diesel-hydraulic locomotives. Indeed a Type 1 engine was used by English Electric Co Ltd to

The bogie used for the HB electro-diesels was a modified version of that used for the HA straight electric locomotives. In this view the retractable shoe gear is in the down position, Class 47 Preservation Project Archive

test the prototype HB propulsion system. However due to differences in the locomotive installations some modifications were required for this purpose and these had to be reversed after completion of the tests so that the engine in question could become a Type 1 spare. This was why a separate contract was raised to supply the engine for trial purposes. There were costs involved in modifying and testing the engine at Colchester, and then reverting back to the Type 1 form after the engine returned to Colchester from English Electric.

A spare engine ordered for the Western Region locomotives, No 640012/4, was initially supplied for the HB locomotive project, under Paxman Contract 58658 dated 22 April 1965. Under this contract, the engine was converted to HB locomotive build standard and sent to English Electric's Newton-le-Willows Works for testing the prototype of the HB locomotive's propulsion system. After testing was completed, the engine was returned to Paxman and converted back to diesel-hydraulic locomotive build before being despatched in fulfilment of Contract 58124.

The essential differences were as follows.

1. The Type 1 engine drove a hydraulic transmission with the engine speed running at 600rpm when idling to a maximum of 1,500rpm. They were fitted with a Max-Min governor which controlled these two speeds. The engine speed in between was controlled by the driver, giving engine speed control much like that of a road vehicle. The HB engines by comparison, drove a DC generator and ran at a constant speed of 1,500rpm. This required a constant speed governor to be fitted. Thus whilst the governors fitted to the engines were similar they had different internal builds. (This also explains why, with the diesel engine operating on the HB type and the associated noise, some drivers later referred to the type as 'spin-dryers'.)

2. The Type 1 engines sat on anti-vibration mounts to minimise engine vibrations transferred to the locomotive. The engines in the HB locomotives had their generators mounted rigidly on a sub-frame which in turn sat on anti-vibration mounts. This different arrangement would also change the feet on which the engines sat and the couplings between the engines and their respective driven machinery.

3. The Type 1 engine was fitted with an electric starter motor for starting the engine. In comparison, the HB locomotive engines drove a DC generator which could be run as a motor to start the engine and so did not require a separate starter motor.

As part of the conversion work, 11 Paxman Ventura 6YJXL engines were purchased. These were supplied under Paxman Contracts 58891 to 58900, dated 11 November 1965. Interestingly, the order was placed not by British Rail, but instead by the English Electric Company Ltd's Dick Kerr Works at Preston. The contracts were for the supply of the complete generating sets, with the generators supplied to Paxman by English Electric. The engines used were Nos 640012/11–12, 650005/1–7, and 650025/1. The complete engine and generator sets were then delivered to Crewe works between September 1966 and July 1967. A spare engine and generator set was supplied by Paxman under Contract 58964 dated 19 June 1966, using engine No 650038/1. This was sent to Eastleigh works in October 1967, suitably packed for long term storage.

The engine radiator bank, along with the EE766/1B Radiator Fan Motor, exhaust ducts and silencer were placed in the space left by the removal of the pantograph well.

Multiple Working Capability

On the cab fronts the standard Southern Region EMU jumper cables and brake pipes were added. The bufferbeam was modified with the addition of buckeye couplings and Pullman rubbing plates, and the original fairing around the buffers was removed. A BR pattern ETH jumper cable and socket was fitted in place of the original UIC pattern plug and socket.

Whilst the HB electro-diesels could operate in multiple with most of the SR's locomotive fleet, there were some restrictions, multiple-working not possible with the JA type electro-diesels Nos E6001-E6006. Where a JB type electro-diesel and an HB type or indeed where two HB types to be coupled together for multiple-working only one of the two locomotives could use electric power. The HBs only could work in multiple with the push-pull fitted BRCW Type 3 diesel-electrics.

The Electrical Equipment

The electrical equipment was supplied by English Electric Co Ltd under contract No CCT1414. Some equipment was new, other items modified, whilst the traction motors for example remained unaltered.

Provision was made for ETH and this could be supplied to the train when operating under both electric or diesel power; this was unlike the smaller JA and JB type electro-diesels which could only provide electric heating when running on electric power, or when pre-heating on diesel power.

Auxiliary Alternator

The auxiliary alternator used was the EE910/2C. This was a conversion of the EE910 auxiliary generator. The conversion work consisted of removing the six inter-poles and their associated cabling. These were replaced by new brushgear and the six main pole assemblies reconnected. The armature was mounted on the booster generator shaft, while the brushgear fitted to the endplate was fitted to the alternator. Access to the slip-rings and brushgear was via removable covers. Its rating was 85 volts, 75 amps at 1,650rpm. The booster set provided the ventilation and the machine's overall weight was 650lb.

Attached to the endplate was an EE M423 control alternator. This was a three-phase machine which supplied the firing circuits of the thyristor amplifier for the static control of the booster generator field. The correct functioning of the control amplifiers was dependent on the output voltages of this alternator and the auxiliary alternator being synchronised.

Main Generator

For the conversion work, English Electric supplied BR with 12 generators of two slightly different types. Four were the EE 843/B, the other eight the EE 843/C. The EE843 was a six-pole machine, supported at the commutator end by a roller bearing, the opposite end being attached to the Paxman engine. The six main field pole assemblies incorporated the main winding, the starting winding, and the self-excited winding. The auxiliary windings were incorporated in the six auxiliary pole assemblies. The only difference between the two types was the resistance of the battery field windings.

Ventilation was by means of a fan fitted at the driven end of the machine. Air was drawn in at the commutator end and expelled through apertures at the opposite end. The machine's rating was 630 volts, 725 amps at 1,500rpm. The weight in working order was 4,260lb.

When being overhauled the engine and generator were to be retained as a pair wherever possible as there could be alignment problems after the interchange of separate items. If it proved necessary to separate an engine and main generator, the region's CM&EE Inspectorate had to be notified in advance of the work taking place.

The Booster Set

Very little alteration was made to the booster set. As the flywheels were not essential to the converted locomotives they were removed. In their place was the traction motor cooling air fan which meant the traction motor blower unit could be removed to make space for the diesel engine and generator set. The booster set was repositioned, being moved towards the number one end of the locomotive.

The Control System

A new control system was devised for these converted locomotives. The driver's controller had four notches, the same as the remote control train line notches. A further low-power notch was provided for use when shunting. This feature was not available when the locomotive was being driven remotely.

Each notch provided a pre-determined traction motor current along with a finite level of maximum performance. For each control notch there was a control voltage signal either directly from the controller or from the train-line relays if the locomotive was being used on a push-pull service remotely.

This control voltage signal controlled the booster generator field, which was fed through control amplifiers to a thyristor amplifier. This arrangement provided phase angle control of the thyristors in a three-phase bridge and rectified the alternating current supplied by the auxiliary power alternator that was coupled to the booster set shaft. The magnitude of the control amplifier signals altered the thyristor timing angle.

The line volts from the third-rail supply were applied across the whole circuit with the traction motors connected in series parallel. The voltage across them was controlled by the generator output, which either opposed (bucked), or assisted (boosted) the line voltage. The field was driven to 'full buck' prior to starting a positive signal which was derived from the difference between the line voltage and that of the booster generator. Logic circuits were used to control the selection of weak field and reversion to full field. The control system also contained automatic wheelslip detection and correction, as had been developed during the tests using No E5013.

Batteries

Different batteries were fitted in the converted locomotives compared to those used originally. The new ones were from EPS Battery Co Ltd and were their lead acid RSKA type with 48 cells.

Route Availability

With their axle weight of at least 21 tons 5cwt, the HB locomotives had a Route Availability of 7 compared to the previous 6 for the HA locomotives they were converted from and were therefore the highest rated of all the Southern Region's mainline locomotive fleet. With the South Western mainline classified as Route Availability 8 this did not cause too many problems and only a few routes were specifically barred to them.

Standard Southern Region multiple-unit and brake pipes were added to the cab fronts.
1. – Multiple Control Jumper Cable,
2. – High Level Air Brake Pipe
3. – High Level Main Reservoir Pipe
4. – Multiple Control Jumper Receptacle
5. – High Level Air Brake Pipe
6. – High Level Main Reservoir Pipe
7. – ETH Jumper Socket
8. – Air Brake Pipe
9. – Vacuum Brake Pipe
10. – Drawhook, Buckeye Coupling and Rubbing Plate
11. – Train Air Brake Pipe
12. – Main Reservoir Pipe
13. – ETH Jumper Cable

Class 47 Preservation Project Archive

Electro-Diesel Operation

Before any movement on electric power, the locomotive had to be completely over the conductor rail and clear of all unramped connections. When working on electric power and moving into a non-electrified area, the diesel engine needed to be started beforehand and the collector shoes raised before leaving the conductor rail supply. The changeover, either way, could be done whilst the locomotive was moving.

Spares

In April 1967, the issue of spare parts for the new locomotives was considered again and a shopping list of requirements drawn up. Some of what was needed was new, the remainder would be transferred over from holdings for the HA electric locomotives.

Livery

Work started on devising a livery for the converted locomotives at Brighton at the end of December 1965, with the drawing office producing the first painting diagram. This was sent to the CE (T&RS) J. F. Harrison on 26 May 1966 requesting his instructions regarding the livery and badges for the locomotives. The cab-mounted jumper cables could potentially have an impact on the yellow panel's size.

The BR Board agreed the new blue livery on 9 June and shortly after, Harrison passed on the drawings from Brighton to J.B. Bloomfield of BR's Industrial Design Department. Harrison asked for advice on applying the new livery and the location of the BR symbols. The cab-mounted jumper cables were to remain black, given the impracticalities of painting them yellow. Final details though of the cab front's livery were not finalised until September 1967 as the first locomotive neared completion.

At first, the locomotive numbers were placed at both ends. Given the position of the ventilators for the resistance banks, the number at the number one end on the secondman's side had to be placed higher. Locomotive data panels were added from June 1968 onwards. The original livery specification included for the bogies to be painted black with yellow axleboxes with a red stripe through them. All the locomotives were painted this way at Crewe although this was changed to all over black at subsequent overhauls undertaken either at Crewe or Eastleigh.

The conversion work proved protracted and locomotive deliveries to the Southern Region ran very late. Freshly completed at Crewe, No E6101 awaits delivery. Of note are the OHLE warning plates attached to the cab handrails. When painted at Crewe after conversion the axleboxes were painted yellow with a red stripe. At subsequent overhauls they were painted black. *Class 47 Preservation Project Archive*

HB Electro-Diesel Main Spares Requirements, April 1967

Description	2500/650hp Electro-Diesel Locomotives			Remarks
	Spares transferred from electric locomotives	Additional Spares to be ordered	Total Spares Provision	
Bogies complete with wheels, axles, traction motors, and brake gear.				The two bogies being transferred will need to be fitted with shoe gear.
No 1 End	1	0	1	
No 2 End	1	0	1	
Wheels and axles complete with SLM flexible drive	4	0	4	
Traction motor drive – SLM flexible	1	0	1	
Traction Motor Type EE532A	3	0	3	
Traction Motor Armatures	1	0	1	
Air Compressors Type DHC 3	1	0	1	
Exhausters Reavell Type FRU5 ¼ x 10in, complete with EE motor type EE750/12J and with standage coupling to Consolidated Eng. & Brake Co. Ltd Drg E37126	0	2	2	
Exhausters Reavell Type FRU5 ¼ x 10in, complete with EE motor type EE750/11H 110 volt	0	2	2	
Motor Generator Sets (Boosters) EE 836/1B	0	1*	1*	*EE type not known but will be modified version of EE 836/1B booster.
Control Cubicle	–	–	–	
Control Cubicle No 1.	–	1	1	
Control Cubicle No 2.	–	1	1	
Diesel Engine Paxman 6XYL + EE 843B Generator	–	1	1	
Generator EE 843B	–	1	1	
Auxiliary Generator	–	1	1	Will be a modified version of EE 910/1B
Auxiliary Generator Armature	–	1	1	Will be a modified version of EE 910/1B

8
The HBs' Arrival on the Southern Region and into Service

Once completed, No E6101 underwent a series of tests at Crewe before it could be delivered to the Southern Region. These did not go well as during an initial test in mid-September 1967 the diesel engine's silencer and radiator both failed. This required the design of both items to be modified, so putting back the locomotive's possible release from Crewe until the end of September. Even this date proved optimistic and a progress report to the Main Workshops Committee on 23 September indicated that the first locomotive would leave Crewe during the week ending 14 October with the second following on two weeks later during the week ending 28 October. On 1 October No E6102 had reached the Paint shop and was in primer, with No E6103 in base paint. The first locomotive, No E6101, had been painted and was parked in the Diesel Test roads at Crewe. In the Erecting shop No E6104 was nearing completion, No E6105 had been fitted with its traction equipment and work was well advanced on locomotives Nos E6106 and E6108. The remaining three locomotives, Nos E6107, E6109, and E6110, were still at the bodyshell stage of the conversion work.

By mid-October though, neither locomotive had left Crewe. The silencers and radiators had both been modified however but this time the newly installed electronic control system had failed to function. As a result no delivery date could be given until English Electric had overcome these defects. The end of October saw No E6102 still in the Paint shop, classmate No E6103 was now in primer whilst No E6101 was reported to be ready for despatch and was stood in the paint shop yard. In the Erecting shop, No E6105 was almost complete, No E6106 had been fitted with its traction equipment, and No E6107 was partially complete. The bodyshells of the last three locomotives had been completed and were now awaiting fitting out.

Eventually the first HB locomotive, as they were designated after conversion, to arrive on the Southern Region was No E6102 on 5 November 1967 followed a month later by No E6103 on 10 December. Both were formerly allocated to 70D (Eastleigh – 'steam' depot codes were still being used at that time), although upon arrival all the HBs went to Stewarts Lane where they were used on a variety of test trains before gradually entering service.

No E6104 had reached the paint shop at Crewe by 29 November and been painted, though not yet numbered. Also present were No E6105 in primer and No E6106 in base paint. No E6103 had been painted and been returned to the Erecting shop. The partially completed No E6107 was also there along with No E6108 which had now been fitted with its traction

Above: **The last of the converted locomotives, No E6110 stands at Bournemouth station soon after arrival from Crewe. Judging by the locomotive's condition it can only have been a matter of weeks after its completion.** *Class 47 Preservation Project Archive*

equipment. The final two locomotives, Nos E6109 and E6110, were still just bodyshells at this stage. The first locomotive, No E6101, was also to be found in the arrivals siding at Crewe having returned there for attention.

In his report to the BR Board submitted on 20 December the CE (T&RS) A. E. Robson said that the control equipment issues had now been resolved, subject to line testing on the Southern Region in mid-January. When these tests have proved the equipment, modifications will have to be made to the six locomotives completed already by Crewe.

On 29 January 1968, No E6102 was used on a test train with a Driving Trailer from 4TC unit No 403 on the Alton branch. By early February the control system on No E6101 had been modified and was now working. This locomotive was then used for a series of tests to reduce engine silencer noise. There were a further three completed locomotives at Crewe, all of which were awaiting modifications by English Electric.

Work was completed at Crewe on Nos E6104 to E6106 and on 4 February they were in the paint shop having been painted, whilst No E6107 was in primer. On the test road was No E6101, whilst in the Erecting shop, No E6109 was nearly complete and No E6110 had had its traction equipment installed. Also seen there that day was No E6108 which was still to be painted.

Numerically the first locomotive, No E6101, did not arrive on the Southern Region until 11 February 1968. It started trial running on the South Western Division at the end of February. Availability statistics dated 14 February 1968 showed just two of the type in stock locomotives in stock, but neither was available for traffic as they were both undergoing maintenance.

On 18 February No E6102 took DTSO No 76331 from Stewarts Lane to Hither Green. All that week they were used on tests, along with 35 hopper wagons, that ran from Hither Green to Folkestone and Dover returning via Chatham and Dartford. On 21 February during one of these tests, the locomotive ran on its diesel engine between Maidstone East and Ashford. The maximum speed for these trains was 55mph. After the journey on Friday 22 February, No E6102 was used to propel the DTSO back to Stewarts Lane.

The fourth locomotive, No E6104, left Crewe on 28 February at 12.05. Running under its own power, it arrived at Stewarts Lane some five hours later at 17.26.

By the middle of March, four locomotives had been delivered. Of these, two had been fully modified, with the other to be modified on the Southern Region. During the week ending 9 March, the fifth locomotive, No E6105, had been on test at Crewe. Two more locomotives had been completed at Crewe and were awaiting modification by English Electric Co Ltd engineers. It was anticipated that the whole locomotive conversion programme would be complete by May, a year later than the original requirement.

During March, on Tuesdays and Fridays, No E6102 was used on a further series of test trains on the South Eastern Division. Its train comprised of either a 4CEP motor coach, 20 coal wagons, and a brake van, or two 4CEP units. On one occasion it is reported that the train failed in the Faversham area.

The BR CE (T&RS) A. E. Robson issued a memorandum on 22 March 1968 on the new diesel and electric classification scheme. So far as the HB electro-diesel locomotives were concerned, from now on they were to be known as Class 74.

Trial running continued during April, six locomotives had been delivered from Crewe. Nos E6107 and 6108 had been modified at Crewe in early April and were undergoing tests. The last two locomotives were reported as being complete and awaiting modification by English Electric and testing before being released to the Southern Region. The last locomotive, No E6110, was in the Paint shop at Crewe on 5 May having been painted.

The Special Traffic Notices prepared each week give us an insight as to the testing regime for each of the Class 74s once they arrived on the Southern Region. For example, Wednesday 1 May 1968 saw No E6107 booked for test runs with No E6108 booked for the same trips on Friday 3 May. On both occasions they were scheduled to leave Stewarts Lane at 09.50 and run light via East Putney to Wimbledon Park Sidings arriving at 10.17. There they would be coupled to two 4VEP EMUs ready for departure at 11.02 heading for Eastleigh Depot. The arrival time was booked for 12.13, entering the depot via the Exit Road, for which special permission had been obtained.

The return working was due to leave Eastleigh at 13.30 arriving at Wimbledon Durnsford Road at 14.33. The two 4VEP EMUs would be uncoupled and the Class HB locomotive would then leave at 15.03 to return to Stewarts Lane light engine running again via East Putney. The arrival time was scheduled for 15.30.

From 6 May, three locomotives were brought into restricted service, mainly on empty stock duties around Waterloo. Gradually their scope of work increased and by the end of June three were being used on passenger duties, one on push-pull trials, and one on crew training runs. This meant that the first of the Brush Type 4s that had been borrowed by the Southern Region in 1966 could be returned to its home depot of Cardiff Canton. In that first week of May, Nos E6104, E6106, and E6107 were all used on boat trains. On 6 May itself No E6106 was used on the 13.16 Waterloo to Southampton East Docks service, in all likelihood the first revenue earning passenger train for the class. An indication of their potential was seen the following day when No E6106 was used on the boat train due to arrive at Waterloo at 21.19; its arrival was eleven minutes early. That week, No E6108 was seen at work on the 09.57 Waterloo to Weymouth Quay as far as Bournemouth, returning to Waterloo with the 15.50 Weymouth Quay to Waterloo which it took over at Bournemouth.

The new locomotives were not without their problems though and as a temporary measure they were taken off freight duties. The automatic acceleration equipment was proving prone to malfunction causing what was described as 'surging' in the train being hauled. This could be unsafe, particularly for freight trains with a potential for goods and coupling damage or even wagon derailment, not to mention discomfort on passenger trains. Ramping circuits were added to slow down the response rate of the control circuits. This is described in greater detail in Chapter 9.

No E6102 shunting stock at Clapham Junction. Closer examination of the photograph shows that the leading wheelset of the front bogie has spoked wheels whilst the other three wheelsets are all solid wheels.
Class 47 Preservation Project Archive

It was at this time that overhauls of the JA, JB, and HB types of electro-diesel were switched temporarily to Crewe from Eastleigh. The reason given at the time was a backlog of work at Eastleigh.

The Class 74s were also used on several railtours during their lives. The first recorded occasion was on 8 June 1968 when No E6108 was used on the Havant to Liss Exchange Sidings section of the Bulleid Pacific Preservation Society's 'Bulleid Commemorative Railtour' to the Longmoor Military Railway. The train had started at Waterloo and had used Southern Railway Co-Co booster locomotives Nos 20001 and 20002 on sections of the journey to Havant. For the return journey to London, No E6108 was used on the section from Liss to Guildford via Haselmere.

July 1968 saw the Southern Region hit by a 'work-to-rule' by drivers and in consequence on the South West Division, the Southampton Docks boat trains were replaced by road transport. The Channel Islands trains to Weymouth continued with a variety of different locomotives used. On 2 July No E6104 with two 4TC sets was used on an Up service having been used earlier that morning to propel the 4TC units as the 8.30 departure from Waterloo.

Generally the type found their main passenger work on the Weymouth boat trains as far as Bournemouth, boat trains to Southampton Docks and some Bournemouth to Waterloo services which had originated off of the electrified network. On 10 August No E6108 was used on the 18.37 Waterloo to Southampton Docks boat train for the Cogedar Line ship *Aurelia*. Ten days later though No E6107 showed there was still work to be done to make the class more reliable when it failed between Southampton and Totton when in charge of the 17.44 Waterloo to Bournemouth train. This was becoming a regular duty for the class along with the 09.30 Waterloo to Bournemouth departure.

The end of July and into the beginning of August saw a spate of failures on a variety of trains, the 06.35 Poole to Waterloo service was particularly badly hit. This train was booked for a Class 33 between Poole and Bournemouth, leaving Bournemouth at 06.57 with the Class 33 having given way to a Class 74 propelling the train. It called at most stations as far as Southampton. Leaving there it called at Eastleigh, Winchester and Basingstoke. The scheduled arrival at Basingstoke was 08.18. The last part of the journey to Waterloo was non-stop, arriving at 09.02.

On 31 July, No E6103 suffered a temporary failure at Southampton which caused a six minute delay. The following week on 5 August, a brake defect on No E6110 meant the train had been terminated at Bournemouth. The next day, No E6107 failed between Shawford and Winchester. The diesel shunter pilot at Winchester was used to rescue the train and haul it to Winchester where it was terminated. There were further problems the next day and whilst the train arrived at Waterloo, it was 34 minutes late from Basingstoke because of problems with No E6109.

Long-suffering passengers then had two weeks respite until 20 August when problems with No E6105 meant it had to be taken off the train at Eastleigh and replaced by Class 33 No D6537. Two days later and again the train locomotive, this time No E6109, was removed at Eastleigh after losing 18 minutes on the journey from Bournemouth.

The return working for this service was the 17.44 Waterloo to Bournemouth, also a regular Class 74 duty and as might be expected was also the victim of problems. On 30 July, No E6106 failed at Southampton Airport with this service. Help came in the form of Class 46 No D151 which was working the 18.05 Salisbury to Northam van train. It took the Class 74 and its train to Southampton Central where the service was terminated. The following day the 17.44 Waterloo to Bournemouth was again terminated at Southampton Central, this time because the train locomotive No E6109 was found to have a loose collector shoe. Just over two weeks later, the service did arrive at Bournemouth, though No E6107 had managed to lose 23 minutes between Southampton and Bournemouth. Two days later the same locomotive failed between Southampton and Totton whilst working the same service.

The 17.44 down had a similar stopping pattern to the 06.35 morning train from Poole. Its journey time as far as

Bournemouth where the Class 74 would give way to a Class 33 was 2 hours 4 minutes. To put this in context the Waterloo to Bournemouth fast service with a 4REP and two 4TC units did the journey in 1 hour 46 minutes, and the semi-fast services were timed at 2 hours and 7 minutes with less stops.

Elsewhere as well the class were having major reliability problems. No E6103 was due to work the 10.44 Southampton Western Docks to Waterloo service on 29 July. However it failed prior to departure and Class 47 No D1984, at the time allocated to Gateshead, had to be used in its place. The service finally left some 70 minutes late. A few weeks later, on 23 August the 11.40 Waterloo to Bournemouth service was terminated at Southampton Central after the failure of No E6101. The following day the 14.47 Swanage to Waterloo was delayed by 50 minutes at Bournemouth following the failure of No E6106. Class 33 No D6513 took over the train.

Crew training continued for a number of months, with locomotives being used for both static and on the road tuition. Early August 1968 was typical of the testing and tuition being undertaken. Saturday 3 August saw a crew training trip booked, using a Class 74 and eight air-braked coaches leaving from Clapham Junction at 10.47 and running via East Putney to Wimbledon and on to Barton Mill carriage sidings near Basingstoke, with an arrival time of 11.57. The return journey was booked for a 13.02 departure from Barton Mill taking the same route back to Clapham Junction to arrive at 14.05.

During the following week of Monday 5 August to Friday 9 August, a member of the class was to be made available for static training at Southampton (Up siding East) between 13.30 and 16.30 each day. That same week there was a crew training trip each day with a member of the class and 10 coaches. Like the Saturday train, this left Clapham Junction at 10.47 and ran via East Putney to Wimbledon. Most of the week its destination was Eastleigh, but on Wednesday the train was booked to go only as far as Basingstoke.

Another locomotive used for testing that week was No E6102. On Thursday 8 August it was allocated to a series of tests between Basingstoke West Yard and Eastleigh Carriage Sidings for the CM&EE. Its train for these tests comprised of spare 4TC DTSO No 76331, a brake van, 35 empty wagons and another brake van. The first trip left Basingstoke at 09.15 arriving at Eastleigh at 10.15.

No E6108 saw further railtour action when it was chosen to haul the LCGB's 'Hampshireman' from Waterloo on 3 November 1968. The Class 74 was used on the legs firstly from London Waterloo–Clapham Junction–East Putney–Wimbledon–Worcester Park–Epsom–Leatherhead–Effingham Junction–Guildford–Haslemere–Havant–Cosham–Fareham, then the section from Totton–Brockenhurst–Bournemouth Central–Poole, Poole–Broadstone–Blandford Forum and return, topped and tailed with Class 47 No D1986. (This tour was featured in article form at Blandford Forum in *Southern Way 38*.)

The 06.35 Poole to Waterloo service suffered problems again on 13 November when the train engine No E6102 failed at Parkstone. It was rescued by No E6109 which took it and its two 4TC units forward to Waterloo.

The derailment on 18 December of part of the 12.20 Didcot to Weymouth van train whilst shunting at Winchester caused

The bay platform at Waterloo was a common place to find a Class 74 as it waited for its next duty. In this case No E6110 is stabled there. In the pre-TOPS era the locomotives' numbers were applied at both ends, though these had to be placed higher at the No 1 end on the assistant's side because of the resistance bank ventilation grilles. *Class 47 Preservation Project Archive*

The Class 74s were allocated to Eastleigh and so were a common sight in the area. No E6106 and another are stabled at Airport sidings.
Class 47 Preservation Project Archive

major disruption for the South Western Division. Amongst others the 17.44 Waterloo to Bournemouth service was diverted via Havant and Netley, with No E6109 hauling two 4TC units on diesel power. Alas, the diesel engine locomotive failed at St. Denys just short of the conductor rail causing further disruption to services that night.

The Class 74s' reliability had not improved much by the start of 1969, in service failures were still frequent although one plus point was that they were now permitted to be used on freight duties. The 17.44 Waterloo to Bournemouth passenger service was still a regular for them, though often worked by a Class 33 diesel or Class 73 electro-diesel due to continued Class 74 failures. In a change to previous operation, the two 4TC units used on this service were now hauled from Waterloo rather than propelled as had been the case.

The south of England was hit by very heavy snow in February 1969, causing major disruption. On 19 February the 22.35 Weymouth to Waterloo service left as normal, but arrived some 5½ hours late in London the following day due to heavy snow and the failure in the Farnborough area of the Class 74 hauling the train.

Due to engineering work on 9 March, single line working was in operation between Allbrook and Eastleigh over the down fast line. Whilst running over this section, the 14.42 Weymouth to Waterloo service failed with electrical trouble on 4REP unit No 3006, Class 74 No E6107 sent from Eastleigh to push the failed train to Winchester. The following day, No E6108 failed at Totton with the 15.30 Waterloo to Swanage service. Class 33 No 6508 which was being used on the 12.20 Didcot to Weymouth parcels train was taken off and used to propel the Swanage train as far as Bournemouth where the service was terminated.

Despite these continuing problems, the Class 74s were being entrusted to some special workings. No E6103 was used on a special comprised of two 4TC units on 21 March back from Southampton where participants had been to view the new *Queen Elizabeth 2* ocean liner. The stock arrived at Waterloo in time to form the 17.44 service to Bournemouth. However Class 73 No E6034 was attached to the front of the train prior to departure, such was the Southern Region's reluctance to use the Class 74s to propel trains over long distances at the time.

The railway press also reported at this time, that at least two of the class, Nos E6103 and E6105, had had their headcode roller blinds changed to ones which displayed a black character on a white background.

Reliability continued to be a problem. On 8 April No E6109 failed at Micheldever whilst working the 12.32 Poole to Clapham Junction empty van train. Classmate No E6102 was sent from Basingstoke to rescue the stranded train.

Instances at this time of Class 74s straying off of the South Western Division were rare, so it was of some surprise when No E6110 appeared at Norwood yard on 19 April, the first recorded appearance of the class at this location.

The LCGB's 'Woodpecker' railtour was run on 22 April 1969 from Waterloo to the HP Bulmer Ltd site at Hereford. For the first part of journey to Reading No E6101 was used. At Reading

No E6108 waits to leave Waterloo on 22 April 1969 with the LCGB's 'Woodpecker' railtour. The electro-diesel took the train as far as Reading where Class 43 No D854 *Strongbow* took the train onto Hereford. *Class 47 Preservation Project Archive*

it gave way to Class 43 Warship No 847 *Strongbow*, an appropriate choice of locomotive, given the tour's destination.

No E6109 was in trouble again on 7 May when it failed in the Weybridge area, this time the problem was a lost collector shoe.

The newly-completed ocean liner *Queen Elizabeth 2* continued to attract attention at Southampton and was visited by a party from the Council of Industrial Design on 29 May. The party travelled down by special train which consisted of 11 new Mark 2b coaches supplemented with two Mark 1 buffet cars. Pleased to report that for this prestige duty Class 74 No E6105 satisfactorily worked the train from Waterloo to Southampton in both directions.

For a change on 19 August, a Class 74 was used to rescue a failed train rather than itself having to be rescued. Class 33 No 6528 was hauling the 18.10 Waterloo to Salisbury when it failed at Clapham Junction. Class 74 No E6102 was used to take the train on to Basingstoke, where Class 33 No 6545 took over for the remainder of the journey westwards.

Another ongoing issue with the Class 74 locomotives was their tendency to catch fire. This happened at Hook on 7 September with No E6107 when working a down 'Ocean Liner Express' to Southampton. A class 33, No 6524, was removed from a freight train in order to rescue the passenger working. It took the failed train to Basingstoke where No E6107 was removed and No 6524 took the train on to Southampton.

Another incident was when No E6109 managed to become derailed at Bournemouth Central, obstructing the down line. As a result single line working had to be put in place that evening between Bournemouth and Christchurch with considerable delays to traffic in both directions. Then just before Christmas it was No E6107's turn to cause problems. It was being used on the 06.52 Eastleigh to Basingstoke service when it failed at Micheldever. The 06.20 Bournemouth to Waterloo service, which was following it, had to be used to push the failed electro-diesel and its train through to Basingstoke.

9
Class 74 Technical Problems

During the course of their brief lives in service the Class 74s suffered from a number of technical problems which impacted both on their availability and their miles per casualty statistics. Interestingly, W. J. A Sykes in his paper to the Institution of Mechanical Engineers in December 1968 entitled 'The Bournemouth Electrification' said that from an engineering point of view, conversion of existing locomotives had been unwise.

Early problems with their electronic equipment were caused mainly by either voltage spikes from neighbouring circuits, some faulty components, and maintenance staff unfamiliar with the equipment they were being asked to maintain. Indeed the system's design meant it could be extremely misleading when diagnosing and then correcting faults, so leading to longer times out of service. Individual pieces of equipment would test correctly but when used in combination would then indicate a fault. Fault finding was with plug-in equipment and early worries even concerned the reliability of the actual test equipment.

Of the main locomotives in the BR fleet, the Class 74s were when introduced, along with the Class 50 diesel-electrics, the only locomotives to be fitted with electronic Over Voltage Protection and electronic Wheel Slip Protection. Furthermore the Class 74s were BR's first locomotives to be controlled mainly by electronic devices. This was at a time when the demands on such equipment fitted in locomotives and rolling stock were not appreciated fully.

G. G. Kibblewhite from the British Rail HQ Staff studied the use of locomotive electronics and the results were published in 1969 in his paper 'British Railways Experience with Electronic Control Gear on Locomotives: 1966/68'. In the section on the Class 74s he said that in a period of six months there were no less than 50 failures of their electronics. As a result of these problems considerable modifications had to be incorporated into the original design. These have included replacement of components and making changes to circuits in order to deal with the problems that had arisen. The Mean Time Between Failure rate was around 10,000 hours. Mean time between failures (MTBF) describes the expected time between two failures for a repairable system. Kibblewhite said that this level of failure in the early months of Class 74 operations indicated the development work on the class was insufficient.

Above: **Despite their poor reliability record to begin with, the Class 74s were given several peak hour trains, to and from Waterloo. On one such train is No E6108. This locomotive was recognisable for a while with its red painted brake pipe holders**
Class 47 Preservation Project Archive

The Class 74s were allocated to Eastleigh for the whole of their service lives. The depot played a vital role in keeping them 'on the road'. Here No 74008 undergoes maintenance inside the main depot building. *Class 47 Preservation Project Archive*

To be fair this had not been helped as the timescales for the Bournemouth scheme were particularly tight to begin with. The delays in the supply of various items of electrical equipment from English Electric had added to the problem. This meant that the testing and development of the various component parts and how they performed together had to be shortened considerably. It was clearly not feasible to delay the whole Bournemouth scheme to ensure these locomotives were reliable from the start, but as has been seen it did mean that in the early months of service, the Class 74s reliability and availability was nothing short of disastrous.

The design problems can be summarised as a combination of several factors. There were mistakes of rating of equipment, the wrong choice of components, insufficient resistance to surge, and poor circuits. The environmental conditions the equipment was placed into, such as temperature, water, and dirt, all had a major impact on its reliability. The third key factor was the complexity of the equipment was unnecessary. These problems when added to a certain level of manufacturing defects and defective components were some of the reasons why the class's early reliability was so poor.

The Class 73s by comparison had begun as a prototype batch of six locomotives that were tested and used in service extensively before the main build of 43 locomotives was started. This meant all the main bugs and gremlins were identified and dealt with well in advance.

Problems with the Class 74s began at Crewe during the conversion work. One key aspect of the electronic equipment design was the use of plug-in card assemblies. Such techniques were already commonplace in the aircraft and other industries. In the railway environment this was new territory with a consequential lack of expertise in the necessary design and installation methods. This meant for example that the plug-in cards were not located securely and fell out of place whilst the locomotive was in use, resulting in a locomotive failure.

During the initial locomotive testing after completion at Crewe it was found that the locomotive would not work in multiple with another electro-diesel. A strange result as multiple-working with other locomotives had been a key Southern Region requirement.

The original 33-notch control was replaced by solid state electronic equipment. This enabled the driver to select any accelerating current value desired, and therefore tractive effort, that was less than the overload relay setting. That tractive effort value would then be maintained up to the performance level.

However, during the locomotives' long and drawn out testing phase it was found, given the train loads the locomotives would be used on, that a revised and simplified control system was required. This was much similar to the system used on the region's multiple-unit stock

One key characteristic of the four-notch control system that was finally used on the class was the rapid response of the equipment when the controller was moved from, for example, notch one to notch four. This could produce a change in the locomotive's tractive effort in excess of 100% in as little as 0.3 seconds. This had the effect of causing traction surges throughout the train and was a major problem when the locomotive was being used on an unfitted freight service. To mitigate the problem and reduce the rate of rise in traction motor current, the so called 'ramping' circuits were introduced into the control logic.

The response speed in controlling the locomotive's output power all impacted upon the booster motor circuit. In certain circumstances it could cause unnecessary operation of the current limiter protection. Once the booster equipment reached its maximum, the locomotive's traction motors operated on their own natural characteristics. As a result an error signal was created between the control signal and the feedback signal. This meant there was a reduced response to any wheelslip at high speeds. However, until the booster had reached its maximum output, the wheelslip control was excellent, being capable of arresting a slipping axle within half a wheel revolution.

Unlike the Class 73 electro-diesels, the Class 74s were not equipped with electro-pneumatic brakes for use with multiple-unit stock. It was an option considered, but it was felt the amount of time the 10 locomotives would be working with such stock did not justify the added cost of its installation. Whilst the locomotives' air brakes proved satisfactory with locomotive hauled stock, problems were found when the class were used with EMU stock. The air brakes in such circumstances were found to lack flexibility, most notably when the locomotive was at the rear of the train propelling.

There was a tendency for logic-box crystals to overheat and a range of replacements were tried. Adding cooling fins in their enclosures would have added additional weight to already heavy locomotives.

Many of the other problems associated with the use of solid-state equipment in locomotives arise with the interface between solid-state logic and electro-mechanical logic. With the Class 74s, the traction output utilised solid-state control, with the rest being under electro-mechanical control.

The locomotives' uneven weight distribution was the cause of further problems. The No 2 end was slightly heavier by 2 cwt, in consequence poor track conditions could cause the locomotive to rock at times uncontrollably. At its worst, stopping the train was the only way to stop the rocking motion.

Class 74 Annual Variation in Reliability							
	1968	1969	1970	1971	1972	1973	1974
Km x 10³	394	896	830	976	954	965	936
Total casualties		66	91	58	53	53	36
Casualties due to electronic equipment	{164}	10	14	11	7	3	3
Average km/casualty x 103		2.4	13.6	9.1	16.8	18.0	18.2	26.1
Service hours x 103 (estimated)	11.1	25.3	23.5	27.6	26.9	27.3	26.1
Electronic Equipment defects	21	41	30	26	17	15	16
Mean time before failure (m.t.b.f.)	528	617	784	1060	1580	1820	1650
Corrected m.t.b.f.	528	685	940	1230	2690	2730	3310
Theoretical Ratio of m.t.b.f. corrected	106:1	82:1	60:1	46:1	21:1	21:1	17:1

The driver's assistant looks back as No E6106 moves its train of empty stock out of Clapham yard.
Class 47 Preservation Project Archive

Availability problems were such that in April 1969, it was being reported that only three locomotives were available to work eight diagrams. For example on 12 April Nos E6101, E6102, E6107, and E6109 were all at Eastleigh depot out of use. A visitor to the depot some three months later on 20 July saw Nos E6106, E6108, E6109, and E6110 all stabled there.

Even if locomotives were not failing completely, the unreliability of the electrical equipment would cause problems. On 4 November 1969, No E6102 was used on the 06.52 Eastleigh to Basingstoke service. It failed at Shawford with an electrical problem, which after some considerable delay the driver managed to rectify and the train continued its journey. Low availability however continued through much of the year with by the end of 1969 an average of only three locomotives a day being ready for use.

Although after several years in service, with experience gained, their reliability improved, it still was less than comparable locomotives. In the four weeks ended 4 November 1972, there were three Class 71 casualties out of the 14 locomotives in service. The Class 74s also suffered three casualties over the same period, compared to the Class 73s where there were five for the 48 locomotives in the class.

Even in their last full year of service, availability could be poor despite the great strides that had been made to improve their reliability, for example on 20 February 1977 only No 74008 was available for traffic.

The Paxman Engine

Although the actual annual running hours for the Paxman engines were low, they were started up and run for short periods fairly frequently. When taking over a locomotive, the Driving Instructions specified that the diesel engine should be started first even if electric power was available. The first movement of the locomotive should be on diesel power before switching to electric. However, if the locomotive had only been shut down for a short time then it could be moved straightaway on electric power.

This meant that whilst the engine running hours were relatively low, around 500 per year on average, the hours that the engines stood with hot coolant in them were very much higher compared to other engines. This resulted in a fairly rapid deterioration of the 'O' ring seals in the cooling system compared to the engine running hours. This was due to the material used, Nitrile Rubber, which deteriorates over time when in contact with hot coolant. As a result they suffered from coolant leaks which in turn could lead to engine failures due to low coolant levels. Some seals were replaced later on with ones made from Viton Rubber. This is a far more durable material and would have been what we would now use today on newly designed engine cooling systems. This infrequent engine use also caused the cylinder heads to fracture so necessitating works repairs.

Starting the locomotives meant the Paxman engine had to be started first. This was done in the usual way and once running it was used to create the required pressure in the main air reservoir. When sufficient pressure was reached, a switch was closed which allowed the booster to start. The engine coolant system was electronically controlled and the whole operation depended on the header tank to be full or close to full.

The problems in starting the Paxman engine continued throughout their lives. One way around the problem was by using the locomotives' pre-heating capability, which was more properly used for providing train heating when the locomotive was unmanned. With the master switch in the 'OFF' position, the pre-heat switch would be switched on. Around one minute later, the Paxman engine would start. With the engine running, the locomotive's air pressure would rise and on reaching the required level, the booster would start. The engine would then pick up speed until the maximum rpm was reached. At this point, and it has to be said, against the driving instructions, the master switch would be moved to either 'FORWARD' or 'REVERSE' depending on the required direction of travel.

The Paxman engine drew complaints from train crews regarding both its noise and the vibration it produced. Indeed, locomotive vibration was a major cause of equipment malfunction. Tests were carried out during 1970 and 1971 with No E6105, in an attempt to find a solution. The generator brush gear was modified by making it considerably stiffer than the original arrangement. The engine and generator bedplate was also fitted with stiffer rubber mountings. These modifications were found to have detuned the system and reduced the transmission of relative motion between the locomotive body and the engine and generator set.

Maintenance – 1968-1972

In contrast to the Class 71s, the Class 74s were not always maintained at Eastleigh. A backlog of work there meant that between their introduction into service in 1968 and 1971, overhauls were undertaken at Crewe. The Class 73s were similarly affected. The locomotives usually travelled there under their own power over the West Coast Mainline in both directions.

The suggested repair schedule for the Class 74s was for Intermediate repairs to be carried out on the locomotive body, engine, and generators after 250,000 miles or 4,000 hours of operation. General overhauls would be undertaken after 500,000 miles or 8,000 hours of operation. The bogies and traction motors would be given classified repairs no matter what the type of overhaul being carried out.

Consequently during this period there are a number of reports of Class 74s undergoing overhauls and other heavy maintenance at Crewe. Just a year into its service life, No E6104 was noted in the Electric traction shop at Crewe undergoing attention on 13 April 1969. Three months later, on 27 July No E6109 was at Crewe in the new Erecting shop, before the following week moving to the Electric shop. Two weeks before Christmas 1969, on 14 December, No E6102 was there undergoing attention in the Electric traction shop. Towards the end of January 1970, it was joined there by No E6103, Indeed there seems to have been a steady stream of Class 74s making the journey north in the first part of 1970 because on 26 April No E6106 was noted in the Electric traction shop. It had been seen on 1 April at Lichfield on trial along with Class 73 No E6022.

Following the Chertsey collision (see page 83) No E6109 was taken to Crewe for repair. It was there for a number of months as the damage was repaired. It was first noted in the Electric traction shop in July. There it remained, being joined by No E6107 which was seen in the arrivals sidings at Crewe on 23 August. The pair were then noted in the Electric traction shop on 27 September. No E6109 was not ready for release back into traffic until late December; it was seen in the test road on 20 December.

Noted in the arrivals siding at Crewe works on 14 March 1971 was No E6105. It had arrived two days earlier having been seen passing Bletchley heading north running on diesel power. It was noted heading south again passing Northampton on 21 July. However, it was soon back again at Crewe for repairs as on 31 October it was seen in the test road at Crewe following attention. In later years, from 1972 until their withdrawal at the end of 1977, overhauls were carried out at Eastleigh.

In Service Experiences

So what were the Class 74s like to live with on a daily basis? Their good points and the main types of problems encountered with the Class 74s can be summarised very well in the reminiscences of John Wenyon and Dave D'Arcy.

The first is of a journey made by John Wenyon, co-author of this book. John takes up the story.

'During the summer of 1969 I was asked to ride on a Class 74 hauled ECS boat train working from Clapham Junction Yard to Southampton Western Docks as a technical representative from the CM&EE department. One of the boat train coach sets was being used for testing experimental brake blocks and other modifications to the brake systems. The presence of a technical rider, when one was available, was supposed to give reassurance to the traffic department.

'Our journey started when the crew reversed the train, on diesel power, out of the sidings, past the carriage washing plant, to gain access to the Down main line, crossing the Up main en route. Having got the signal, the locomotive, with 650hp of power, dragged the train slowly alongside the Down main platform.

'The driver then shut down the diesel set and selected electric power. The result was a deathly silence on board. The driver restarted the diesel engine to at least keep the train moving and avoid coming to a stop in the platform. There was much frantic scrabbling by the driver's assistant inside the locomotive, which was rewarded finally by the announcement that someone had left the air supply to the shoegear isolated. Having dealt with this problem, electric power was then used to very good effect to get the train, which was now 10 minutes late, and blocking the Down main line, up to line speed and out of everyone's way.

'A fast but uneventful journey proceeded, until having passed Basingstoke and approaching Worting Junction at 90mph under green signals, the signal a quarter of a mile ahead suddenly turned red. A sharp intake of breath from the cab's occupants was followed immediately by the driver shutting off power and reaching for the brake valve. Before he could apply the brake the signal turned green again. There was a slight pause, before power was re-applied. The signal turned red again. Power was shut off once more and the signal turned green, again. "I think that we will coast past this one," said the Driver.

'The probable explanation for this would be a problem with the impedance bonds separating adjacent AC track circuits being magnetically saturated by the locomotive's high DC traction return current. This would have caused a shorting out of the adjacent track circuits. Whatever the true cause, for once it was not the locomotive's fault.

'The journey remained uneventful, until that is the train approached Southampton and after passing over the third rail gap at Mount Pleasant level crossing something failed in the control circuitry. Notch 2 power had been selected but the locomotive started accelerating on full power, and ahead was the 15mph curve at Northam…! By that time the traction current had reached 3000+ amps and the acceleration could be felt on board, the Driver had decided enough was enough. He shut off power, raised the shoegear, made a full brake application and started the diesel engine, for the third time in that journey.

'The remainder of the run round Northam curve, through Southampton tunnel, Southampton Central Station and into the Western Docks was painfully slow, perhaps no more than 10mph. I left the train alongside Berth 102 – and I am happy to report that the brakes had performed perfectly!'

Dave D'Arcy first came across the Class 74s as a secondman at Eastleigh in the early 1970s.

He had been trained on the type at Stewarts Lane and also had some limited time on the Class 71 electric locomotives, mainly around Stewarts Lane. Dave recalls the main difference in driving the two types was the main control handle. The Class 71 handle had 33 notches, whilst in comparison, the Class 74 controller had only four and so was compatible with the 4TC sets with which they could run in multiple. The 'on the road' training for both types could be difficult due to their small cabs which were basically full when four people were on board.

Drivers from Eastleigh of course, as well as Waterloo, Basingstoke and Bournemouth men were trained on the Class 74s, though not Woking men. Originally, Feltham based drivers had a degree of knowledge of them, as it was crews from there who had the task of delivering the type, under diesel power, from Crewe when brand new. With all 10 allocated to Eastleigh, the depot was responsible for all the major repairs including to

Class 74 reliability in their early years was poor and in-service failures were frequent. On 7 May 1970, No E6104 failed whilst in charge of the 07.27 Southampton to Waterloo service. The train is seen leaving Surbiton with assistance provided by Class 73 No E6007. *R. F. Ruffell*

their bogies and traction motors. About the only task not undertaken was the changing of the Paxman diesel engine.

He remembered the class as being both extremely fast and capable locomotives. Speeds of 100mph were not uncommon, even uphill with 14 coaches on a Waterloo bound train from Southampton Docks when the three figure speed could be reached at Wallers Ash whilst still travelling uphill! Some Class 74s it is thought were fitted with speedometers calibrated to 125mph. One driver is understood to have reached 120mph with one of the class whilst heading in the down direction.

Running on diesel power the Class 74s were capable of reaching 50 or even 60mph if required, but much would depend upon the load and gradient. They are not known to have ventured beyond Poole much, although they did on occasions travel on diesel power between Eastleigh and Portcreek Junction north of Fratton at which point the third-rail was available again. The lines between Portcreek and Eastleigh and St Denys were not electrified until the mid-1980s, by which time of course the class had long since been withdrawn. There were also times when the Class 74s ventured towards Salisbury and Andover from Worting Junction. One of these occasions was in the final weeks of the locomotives in service.

One of the down sides of the class was that they were somewhat uncomfortable for the train crew. They would set up the 'fore and aft' movement' already described on particular sections of track, one of the worst of these being on Christchurch bank. Another failing of theirs he recalls, was the position of the cab heaters which were located behind the cab doors. As a result, the driver's back would roast whilst his legs would freeze. If a driver was perhaps short in stature they were again not the most comfortable as the position of the seat and Deadman's pedal meant there was little option but to drive standing up.

Unlike the Class 73 electro-diesels, the Class 74s were not known for suffering from flat batteries. If this did occur, the only way of moving one was with another engine either to a point where a shore supply was available, or by coupling to another similar locomotive so that sufficient electric power was then available to lower the collector shoes. Unlike the Class 73s, the Class 74 shoegear could not be lowered manually.

Dave would dispute the poor reliability made claims against the class. His view is that problems were often due to a lack of familiarity, or even laziness on the part of train crews. The example he gives is when changing ends. The correct sequence was to turn off various switches first in order to cut off power to the control circuits. If this was not done, the contacts could burn out quite easily. This done, the master controller could be then moved to the 'Off' position. However, some drivers would simply move the master controller to the 'Off' position and leave the locomotive, without shutting off the current to the control circuits.

It is his view that it was their complexity that let them down, although power wise they were rumoured to have the equivalent power of a Class 86 or 87 AC electric locomotive. If confirmed, it would certainly explain their ability to lift a train to around 100mph on a 1 in 250 adverse gradient.

He well remembers a rumour circulating at one time that English Electric had offered to build 10 brand-new locomotives for less than the cost of the conversions, but this had been turned down by BR. No doubt BR could not be seen to be

Operating on diesel power No 74005 runs light engine through Basingstoke. The filthy exhaust from the Paxman engine was a common occurrence, given its use in short bursts. This was the cause of some of the engine problems encountered. *Class 47 Preservation Project Archive*

withdrawing engines then only a few years old. However that was exactly what of course did happen to the Class 74s and they were laid aside simply because there was no work for them. Despite their electrical complexity there was at least one area where simplicity was the order of the day. Their mileage counters were a simple device located on the end of an axle. A reading was taken every time a locomotive was refuelled.

Once in service, the class were used on boat, van, freight, and passenger workings. For the Southampton boat trains, the Paxman diesel engine was needed not just for propulsion over non-electrified lines but also for warming the stock whilst waiting for passengers to board. With a long train this could take some time, and most drivers were in the habit of walking through the empty stock, turning the carriage heaters to 'full' to achieve maximum effect, especially if the stock had languished in the carriage sidings for a few days beforehand during a cold spell.

In the early 1970s there was a morning Southampton to Waterloo train formed of a Class 74 hauling two 4TC sets, something Dave understood to have been a throw-back to the steam timetable of a few years before. The class also worked as far as Poole on passenger workings. Even with a single 4TC set this could cause difficulties on Poole bank when heading back towards Bournemouth. The uphill gradient here was 1 in 60, and it was not unknown for a Class 74 and its train to be reduced to barely a walking pace through Parkstone station. Any passengers would be easily able to get on or off as the train was moving so slowly. It was a different story of course upon reaching Branksome, as now being on the third-rail the locomotive would accelerate rapidly with such a light load. Provided also the controller was handled sensibly there was not violent shove from behind when working in propelling mode, though this was not always the case. Some of these services though might even have to be banked if they got into difficulties after leaving Poole. Indeed on one occasion Dave was sent out to provide just such assistance when driving a Class 47.

Another of their regular duties was a van train which Eastleigh drivers worked to Clapham. The locomotive then ran light to Waterloo where it was stabled in one of the dock sidings until working the down night mail/newspapers in the early hours of the following morning. Dave recounts this was the problem with the class, by the time the 10 locomotives were available, discounting any reliability issues; the ocean liner traffic had already reduced and there was simply not

For a time after their conversion, until 1972 repair work on the Class 74s was handled by Crewe works. Photographs of them under repair are uncommon, but here No E6101 undergoes an overhaul surrounded by several AC electric locomotives. *Class 47 Preservation Project Archive*

enough work for them. This was particularly noticeable when a batch of four additional 4REP electric units came on stream in 1974. On any given day, there might be duties for perhaps three locomotives, whilst the reminder stood idle. (On one occasion though he also recalls all 10 were laid aside with defects at Eastleigh and none were available.)

There is one particular incident involving one of the class which sticks in Dave's mind to this day. It happened when he worked with Eastleigh driver Pete Bramble on the 18.30 freight from Southampton Docks to South Lambeth. There was crew change on this service at Eastleigh and the crew they relieved mentioned nothing untoward about the locomotive to Dave and Pete as they took over the train, by now running on electric power.

Everything about their journey was normal until they switched over to diesel power at Clapham Junction for the last section of the outward run. Now both men noticed a slight smell of burning on the way to, and later on the return journey from, South Lambeth. This disappeared again at Clapham, until once more they changed over to diesel power at Mount Pleasant on the outskirts of Southampton. The return journey was again destined for Southampton Docks and they were at this stage running early. The burning smell however worsened gradually. A little further on, as they were running gently past Chapel Crossing there was a tremendous bang from the engine compartment. They stopped the train as quickly as possible and, as Dave put it, 'bailed out'.

Realising they would have to get back on board eventually, there was a cautious approach to the locomotive and a look into the engine compartment. This could be done through two porthole type windows so there was no need to open the door into the compartment. What they saw was an engine compartment filled completely with smoke. Unsurprisingly, the locomotive was a complete failure and assistance would have to be provided.

The final part of this story came a few days later. Dave happened to be in Eastleigh works when he was collared by Foreman Harry Frith who chastised him for ruining the locomotive's Paxman engine. It transpired an injector had worked loose and eventually fallen into the relevant cylinder. With the engine itself still turning the component had then been pushed upwards until it smashed its way out of the crankcase, hence the loud bang and smoke filled engine compartment Such an incident was commonly known as 'putting a leg out of bed' and needless to say this case the Paxman diesel engine had to be written off.

10
The 1970s

With the new decade only five days old, the ongoing reliability problems with the Class 74s showed no signs of abating. No E6104 was booked to work the 17.44 Waterloo to Bournemouth service, a regular Class 74 duty at the time. Shortly before reaching its destination, it failed at Pokesdown, causing a 51-minute delay to the service.

These issues would continue, as less than three weeks later, on 23 January, the driver of No E6106 had to use diesel power when working 08.05 Basingstoke to Waterloo service after an electrical problem occurred at Winchfield. At Woking, Class 33 No 6510 was provided to assist the train to Waterloo. Daily availability of the Class 74s at the time was reported as remaining at 'low levels'.

The long-suffering users of the 17.44 Waterloo to Bournemouth service were delayed again on 19 February. The train locomotive, No E6109, failed at Winchester. The 17.46 Waterloo to Bournemouth service following just behind, had to be used to propel the train to Eastleigh.

By comparison, the Class 71s' availability and reliability continued to be good, though there were occasional problems. On 26 February, No E5005 failed at Herne Bay at around 05.15 with a loss of power whilst in charge of the 02.55 Victoria to Ramsgate passenger, parcel, and newspaper service. Fitters arrived around an hour later to see if they could effect a repair and Class 73 No E6037 was sent from Sittingbourne to move the train on to Margate. By the time the electro-diesel arrived, the technical staff had managed to repair No E5005. The traction current was then restored and the train left Herne Bay at 7.24 with No E6037 dead in tow at the rear.

The middle of March saw the need for both the 'Golden Arrow' and 'Night Ferry' trains to be diverted after work was found to be needed on Bridge No 11 between Victoria and Brixton. Locomotive hauled trains were prohibited, meaning both services had to be routed via Stewarts Lane whilst repairs were completed.

During April and early May, No E5001 was used on a series of Guard training trips with the instruction vehicle No DS70155. These covered the South Eastern Division routes from London as far as Maidstone West and Tonbridge.

New timetables for passenger and freight services were introduced on 4 May 1970. On the South Eastern Division, the Class 71s continued to work a number of air braked services between Dover Marine and Hither Green Continental Depot. There were five weekday trains from Dover with four empty workings in return. Whilst most of these trains ran to a schedule of around two hours in either direction, the 11.26 from Dover Marine was much more tightly timed. It was booked to complete the journey in just 1 hour 38 minutes. Sundays saw just two of these services in each direction. The same period saw the Class 71s still involved in the car transporter trains from and to Knowle & Dorridge. As with the previous timetable the locomotive changeover was done at Ashford in both directions. Ditto their passenger and parcel

Above: **No E5014 is stabled with a Class 47 for company at Stewarts Lane. The tail lamp on the Class 71 would indicate it has been towed from somewhere and it is also without its pantograph. In the background are another Class 71 and a rake of three 4CEP EMUs.**
Class 47 Preservation Project Archive

duties remained largely unchanged, athough the 20.40 parcels service from Dover which they had worked as far as Tonbridge was now extended on from Willesden to terminate at Rugby. Whilst the departure time of the 'Golden Arrow' from Victoria remained at 10.30, the departure time for the return journey was changed. Until 25 September it would leave Dover at 18.13, thereafter the departure time was brought forwards slightly to 18.05. These timings applied throughout the week.

On 1 June, No E6109 whilst hauling the 02.40 Temple Mills to Eastleigh freight service was involved in a collision with 2EPB EMU No 5679 at Chertsey. Three wagons were derailed and there was damage to both the locomotive and the EMU. Following the collision, all 10 Class 74 locomotives were withdrawn from service temporarily and by 3 June all of the class, except No E6109, were at Eastleigh for examination of the brake block slack adjusters. They were all released to traffic the following day whilst No E6109 was moved firstly to Feltham before being taken to Crewe for repairs.

Nine days later on 10 June, fire broke out on a bridge across the River Stour between Christchurch and Pokesdown. No E6103 was working the 15.30 Waterloo to Weymouth service that day which had to be terminated at Southampton. The locomotive and stock were used to return to London as the 16.40 Southampton to Waterloo service and then again as the 18.46 departure from Waterloo.

Although Crewe works was carrying out overhauls on the Class 74s, the Class 71s continued to be overhauled at Eastleigh. The oldest member of the class, No E5001, was noted undergoing repair there on 27 June.

Whilst Class 74 reliability at this time was poor, with in service failures a regular occurrence, there were even occasions where the Class 74s were used to rescue or substitute for another locomotive class that had come up short. One instance came on 22 July when No E6104 was used on the 06.55 Bournemouth to Waterloo service in place of Class 73 No E6022 which had failed. The train left Bournemouth 30 minutes late as a result of the late change of locomotive. Three days later the 05.50 Weymouth to Waterloo service was run as two separate portions from Bournemouth using Nos E6105 and E6102 respectively.

A regular Class 71 duty was the 03.00 Victoria to Ramsgate passenger, parcel, and newspaper service. Unusually a member of the class was unavailable for this train on 11 August, a Wednesday, and so Class 33 No 6561 was used instead.

The Channel Islands boat train running between Waterloo and Weymouth was seasonal and usually booked to be Class 74 hauled each way between Waterloo and Bournemouth. Unfortunately, the last 09.57 departure of the season from Waterloo on 10 October powered by No E6103 failed at Southampton. The failed locomotive was replaced by Class 33 No 6552 for the remainder of the journey.

Classmate No E6107 ran into trouble at Basingstoke on 9 November when in charge of the 15.30 Waterloo to Wareham service. As so often, a Class 33, this time No 6503, was used as the rescue locomotive.

A derailment in the goods yard at Basingstoke required the services of the Wimbledon Park breakdown train and No E6107 was used as the motive power. The same locomotive, No E6107, was itself in trouble again on 6 December. Engineering work meant that the 12.47 Waterloo to Weymouth service was formed of No E6107 and TC stock. Unfortunately the locomotive failed before departure, and another Class 33, this time No 6507, had to be used in its place.

At Dover in 1972 several of the class stabled together – Nos E5004, E5005 and E5007. *Class 47 Preservation Project Archive*

A blue locomotive, with blue and grey liveried Pullman cars. This view of the 'Golden Arrow' at Dover Marine taken on 12 February 1972 with No E5006 shows the train its final months of operation before the service was withdrawn in September 1972. Class 47 Preservation Project Archive

Early in the new year, on 7 January 1971, Class 71 No E5002 was seen in the Lewisham area of London propelling the instruction vehicle No DB70155. Ten days later, on 17 January, there were problems with the 'Golden Arrow'. The train had been diverted because of engineering works and soon after departure from Victoria the train locomotive failed just before 11.00 at Nunhead. The train was delayed for an hour whilst a replacement locomotive was brought from Hither Green.

The flexibility of the Class 74s was demonstrated admirably on 3 March. The usual formation for the 12.47 Waterloo to Bournemouth service of a 4REP and two 4TC units had to be changed because of defective tyres on the motor bogies of the allocated 4REP. Instead Class 74 No E6106 was used to propel an 11TC formation.

A slightly unusual combination involving No E5005 (formerly No E5020) and a 4TC unit No 427 was provided for the Southern Electric Group's 'Man of Kent' tour on 11 April 1971. The special ran from Victoria to Ashford via Canterbury West and the Kearnsey loop to visit the Ashford Steam Centre, before travelling on to Sittingbourne. On arrival there, passengers were able to enjoy a trip on the Sittingbourne & Kemsley Light Railway before heading back to Victoria via Canterbury East, Gillingham, and Chatham. This was the first time a 4TC unit had been seen on the South Eastern Division.

Throughout their lives, Dover was always a place to find several Class 71s stabled prior to their next duty. The Easter weekend of 1971 was one such time when Nos E5001, E5003, E5007, E5011, and E5012 could be found there.

The new timetable came into force on 3 May and indicated a slight reduction of work for the Class 71s in this timetable. The 21.15 London Bridge to Dover Priory mail service which they worked from Tonbridge was lost whilst the 'Golden Arrow' reverted to 'summer' and 'winter' departure times from Victoria once more. Until 29 October it would leave London at 10.30, whilst after 1 November this was moved forwards to 09.30. Similarly, there were different departure times from Dover Marine. These were 18.05 until 29 October and 17.13 from 1 November. The train's 'summer' season resumed in both directions on 20 March 1972.

The 'Night Ferry' also reverted to 'summer' and 'winter' departure times. In 'summer' this was 22.00 from Victoria, and in 'winter' it was 21.00. The morning departure from Dover to London remained at the same time all year round.

Weekends were also beginning showing reductions in work for the Class 71s with just two parcels duties on a Saturday: the 09.25 empty stock service from Margate to Bricklayers Arms which previously they had worked throughout, was now only theirs as far as Dover Priory – there a Class 33 took over. The early morning Victoria to Ramsgate passenger, parcel, and newspaper train remained in their hands, as did the portion to Dover when the train divided at Faversham.

There were also some changes for the Class 74s over on the South Western Division. The 06.30 Poole to Waterloo which they often used to work forwards from Bournemouth became a 4REP duty. Instead the 07.25 Southampton to Waterloo train became a regular Class 74 working and was a Monday to Friday duty. Whereas in the previous timetable the 17.44 Waterloo to

Poole weekday train was booked for a Class 74, in this timetable its equivalent became a 4REP and TC duty instead.

A 24-hour strike by crew members of the French ferry ships *Saint Germain* and *Twickenham* meant the Dover to Dunkirk service was cancelled on 24 September. As a result the 'Night Ferry' was cancelled on both the nights of 23 and 24 September. On 25 September when sailings resumed again the train was formed of EMU stock that day.

The 'Night Ferry' was always susceptible to late running on its in-bound journey to London if the ferry service from France ran late. However on 22 November the down service from London was delayed in the Orpington area due to earlier disruption to services from Charing Cross and London Bridge.

The next timetable change was on 1 May 1972. The 'Golden Arrow' and 'Night Ferry' timings were left unaltered. This of course would prove to be the last timetable with the 'Golden Arrow' running, so it ran on the 'summer' timings until it finished at the end of September. The 'Night Ferry' relief trains were still available at weekends as in previous years.

One feature of both the freight and passenger timetables now was the number of light engine movements undertaken by the Class 71s in order to take up their next duty. For example, the locomotive used on the 04.35 Hither Green Continental Depot to Dover Marine service would then run light to Snowdown Colliery. From there it was used on the 08.35 back to Hither Green. One interesting afternoon move saw two Class 71s coupled together run light from Ashford to Margate. One locomotive would then be used on the 18.35 vans to London Bridge, whilst the other would work the 19.00 freight to Hither Green.

The locomotives were still the main motive power for the air-braked services that ran between Dover and Hither Green. This timetable saw the number reduced to four from the five of previous years. The late afternoon service from Dover at 16.15 was the one to be axed.

The Class 71s continued to be used a number of early morning parcels, mail, and newspaper trains: 02.55 to Maidstone West via Nunhead, and 03.00 to Ramsgate via Swanley and Faversham had both been booked Class 71 duties, almost since entering service in 1959. On 6 May 1972 the 02.55 was worked by No E5008 and the 03.00 worked by No E5005.

On the South Western Division the Class 74s retained the 07.25 Southampton to Waterloo service, and its stopping pattern was the same as previously. This timetable like ones before it had provision for a number of conditional trains to and from Waterloo and Southampton Docks. A feature of these trains, all of which were booked for electro-diesels, was that they ran to both Southampton Eastern and

No E5006 arrives in Ashford Downside Reception Siding No 1 with an Up direction mixed freight on 28 March 1972. The headcode 9D indicates a Hither Green Continental Depot to Dover Marine via Chatham train which it clearly is not. In all likelihood that was the previous down working by the locomotive which never got changed when it picked up the mixed freight train. *Stephen Godden*

No E5003 arrives in Ashford Downside Yard with an Up direction mixed freight on 13 March 1972. The headcode 5C indicates a Hither Green to Dover Town via Maidstone East train. This must the return leg as the train is leaving in the Up Direction towards Maidstone East. It is interesting to note the illuminated L sign at low level, an indication to the driver to lower the pantograph and go onto the third rail. *Stephen Godden*

Western Docks with Northam Junction the usual place for the two parts of the train to come together on the run to Waterloo.

Elsewhere the empty stock workings of the 'Golden Arrow' between Victoria and Clapham Junction were usually worked by Class 33 diesels. However on 16 May 1972 Class 71 No E5002 was used instead on the Clapham Junction to Victoria empty stock working. Two days later No E5006 was used, so providing the unusual occurrence of Class 71s at work on the Central Division.

The failure of the 4REP unit No 3011 in the formation of the 15.30 Waterloo to Bournemouth service on 12 June led to No E6104 being drafted in to provide the traction power. The 4REP unit being retained in the train's formation along with the usual two 4TC units.

Over on the Western Region, they were able to obtain No E6104 as an exhibit at the Old Oak Common Open Day held on 2 September 1972. The same month saw Class 71 No E5007 at work around the Ashford area with the instruction vehicle No DS70155.

Changes were made to the freight timetable on 2 October. The main work for the Class 71s was still the air-braked freight trains running between Hither Green Continental and Dover Marine. They were also used on an air-braked service coming up

from Dover going onto Willesden, which the Class 71s hauled as far as Hither Green. An addition to the timetable was an afternoon air-braked duty from Hoo Junction to Dover leaving at 16.16.

Weekends however saw a further reduction in freight activity when compared to previous years. The traffic between Hither Green and Dover consisted of two trains from Dover and one return working. There was also a late morning air-braked duty between Dover Marine and Faversham. Freight activity on a Sunday was even more limited. The only Dover to Hither Green service was the 22.20.

On 25 November No E6109 was seen working over on the London Midland Region at Willesden High Level station with an Inspection train. Five days later, and the same locomotive was used to rescue a failed Class 47 that had been hauling the 05.55 Newcastle to Poole service. The train was seen arriving at Bournemouth with the electro-diesel in charge.

The Final 'Golden Arrow'

The end of the 'Golden Arrow' had been announced in 1971. The last run was on 30 September 1972. The composition of the final train from Victoria was as follows from front to rear: No E5013, S86731 General Utility Van, S4376 Open Second, S4065 Open Second, S25934 Corridor Second, S25944 Corridor Second, S35023 Corridor Brake Second, S3773 Open Second, Pullman car S306S (ex *Orion*), Pullman car S302S (ex *Phoenix*), Pullman car S307S (ex *Carina*), Pullman car S308S (ex *Cygnus*). The same stock was used for the return journey from Dover Marine.

No E5013 was prepared specially for these final two services with the 'Golden Arrow' headboard carried along with the Union Flag and the French Tricolour. To finish off the locomotive, the bodyside golden arrows, not previously used for some time, were affixed to both sides of the locomotive's leading end, and the locomotive ran with white painted buffers.

Unsurprisingly there was much media attention. The footplate crew posed for photographs with the headboard before leaving Victoria, whilst the on board Pullman staff toasted the occasion with champagne at Dover. Independent Television News sent a film crew, and there was coverage in several of the Sunday newspapers the following day including the *Sunday Times*, *Sunday Telegraph* and *The Observer*. With the end of the 'Golden Arrow', Pullman services on the Southern Region came to an end, and of their earlier famed premium services, it was now only the 'Night Ferry' that remained.

1973–1975

One Class 74, No E6104, was fitted with the experimental Southern Region Automatic Warning equipment in addition to the standard AWS fittings. The cubicle housing the equipment for this was located adjacent to the driver's cooker, and so directly above the battery exhauster. The system installed was almost identical to that fitted in the 4REP EMU stock along with the Driving Trailer of a 4VEP EMU. In the driver's cab the 'Signal Approaching' display panel was mounted above the driver's brake valve with the 'Signal Passed' indicator placed

The last down 'Golden Arrow' with No E5013 at the head. The locomotive was well prepared for the occasion and even a set of bodyside arrows were provided to mark the passing of this famous train on 30 September 1972. *John Scrace*

underneath the route indicator box. An electrical horn and bell were provided giving audible signals, the same way as the standard BR system.

The British Rail Technical Committee discussed the use of the equipment and the progress made to date at their meeting on 1 March 1973. The limited trials held to date had not proved the reliability of the equipment or its ability to withstand the rigours of daily use. Although work continued in time the project would be dropped.

Whilst hauling some stock at New Cross Gate on 15 March 1973 No E5014 was in collision with an EMU. Much damage was done to the number one end cab below the handrail level. The damage though was repaired at Eastleigh and the locomotive returned to traffic.

The annual timetable change took place on 7 May. The freight side saw further retrenchment with a reduction in the Hither Green to Dover air-braked services for one. Other services also removed from the timetable were the 16.16 Hoo Junction to Dover service and the Saturday only 11.54 Dover to Faversham.

By comparison the timetable change brought about only minor changes for the Class 74s. Their early morning duty from Southampton to Waterloo was retimed slightly to leave at 07.27 although the arrival time at Waterloo remained at 09.29, a slow schedule for what was in effect a stopping train. This timetable also included four conditional boat trains to Southampton Docks with the possibility of up to seven trains in the opposite direction.

The Class 74s other main duty was the summer dated trains from Waterloo to Weymouth Quay. They ran until 15 October and resumed on 29 April 1974. These trains were worked by Class 74s as far as Bournemouth, with a Class 33 taking over for the journey on to Weymouth and thence the street section over the tramway to the quayside.

The 10.46 Bevois Park to Waterloo parcels service was another train that was usually a Class 74 duty. However, in the summer months of 1973, the Monday train was very often Class 47 hauled instead. Similarly, the Waterloo to Southampton Docks boat trains, again very often worked by the Class 74s, began to see Class 47s used instead. One example of this was on 17 July when the 11.02 Southampton East Docks to Waterloo service was worked by Class 47 No 1523, a Stratford based locomotive at the time and more at home on the Great Eastern mainline.

On 29 August 1973, No E5005 was used on a football special from Dartford to Brighton. The 'League Liner' ran via Bricklayers Arms to Hove taking Charlton Athletic fans to the Third Division match against Brighton & Hove Albion. The Class 71 was used throughout, meaning a rare appearance on the Central Division for a member of the class. The match was won by Charlton Athletic 2-1, although on the way back, the driver forgot to stop at Charlton, meaning an unscheduled stop had to be made at Woolwich Arsenal instead. Fortunately it was in time for the Charlton fans to use the last train home.

Whilst most repair work on the Class 71s was carried out either at their home depot of Ashford or at Eastleigh for more heavy work, there were occasions when repair work was completed elsewhere. On 5 September though, No E5003 was seen under repair at Ashford works.

A few weeks later, and another Class 71 ventured onto the Central Division, this time for the Open Day held at Selhurst on 16 September. No E5011 was one of the locomotives on display.

No E6108 has just arrived at Bournemouth with a mixed rake of stock from Waterloo, including the first vehicle labelled 'Cater for Profit' with what appears to be the Eastern Electricity Board logo on the side. This working took place in June 1973 but so far all enquiries have drawn a blank as to what was its purpose. *Class 47 Preservation Project Archive*

Over on the South Western Division, Class 74 No E6110 was used on a special train chartered by the Ford Motor Co Ltd on 15 October. The four-coach train left Waterloo at 08.03 for Beaulieu Road. On arrival the passengers were taken to the nearby National Motor Museum. The train returned to London at 17.16. Both the locomotive and coaches had the Ford blue oval emblem displayed on them during the day.

Whilst the Class 71's pantographs saw limited use, authority was sought in December 1973 for the purchase of six new ones for them. The total cost was put at £11,280, with a lead time for delivery of 12 months. Approval for this purchase was given by the Investment Committee on 15 January 1974.

Under the TOPS renumbering programme both classes were given five-figure numbers. When renumbered, each class only had the new numbers applied on the driver's side at each end. A depot allocation sticker, either 'AF' for Ashford for the Class 71s or 'EH' for Eastleigh in the case of the Class 74s, was applied below the locomotive data panel and number. In some cases with both the Class 71s and 74s it was possible to see where the old 'E' prefixed number had been painted out on the driver's assistant's side.

The Class 71s were renumbered in December 1973 and January 1974. The Class 74s were altered between December 1973 and February 1974, Nos E6101, E6104 and E6105 being done in December, No E6109 in January 1974, with the remaining six locomotives in February.

One regular duty for the Class 71s was the 03.10 newspaper and passenger service from Victoria to Ramsgate. On 23 April 1974, this train, hauled by No 71005, derailed near Meopham. The train's consist that night was one BSK, three BGs, three PMVs, and three CCTs. The seventh vehicle CCT No M37029, built in 1938, climbed the gauge face of the right-hand rail and one wheelset became derailed on the 6ft side. The train ran through a clipped and padlocked facing point at Sole Street where the other CCT's wheelset derailed on the cess side. Running through a further trailing crossover around 100 yards further on led to all the vehicle's wheels becoming derailed to the cess side. Remarkably, all the wheels re-railed on another trailing crossover a short distance later before the train finally came to a halt. In all, the CCT had travelled 1,826 yards whilst derailed. The subsequent investigation found the cause to be track irregularities, an excessive dip in both rails, causing the vertical unloading of a right-hand wheel.

Left: **No E5012 was quite possibly the last Class 71 to be outshopped after an overhaul with a pre-TOPS number on it. This view shows the locomotive inside Eastleigh Works on 22 October 1973. Two months later it would become No 71012.** *Grahame Arnold*

Below: **No 71010 in its final condition with its five-digit number, now only applied by the driver's side of the cab.**
Class 47 Preservation Project Archive

A few weeks after being renumbered, No 74002 takes some vans out of the Dorset siding, Eastleigh, on 22 February 1974. The filthy exhaust was a common sight with the class when starting a train on diesel power. *Grahame Arnold*

Steam returned to the Southern Region briefly in 1974 when on 27 April No 35028 *Clan Line* worked the Merchant Navy Locomotive Preservation Society's 'Return to Steam on the Southern' railtour from Basingstoke to Westbury and return. The train started from Waterloo and No 74004 was used on this stage of the trip. The same locomotive was used on the return from Basingstoke to Waterloo.

The next timetable change came into use on 6 May as Britain recovered from the three-day week and its after effects. The air-braked traffic between Hither Green and Dover now saw just two trains up from the coast each weekday, with a third going on to Willesden. Saturdays saw just one working each way, and on Sundays there was just the one train from Dover at 21.45. The 11.54 Saturday working of the previous timetable from Dover to Faversham was cut.

On the passenger, parcel, and mail side, the work was also thinning out. There were noticeable reductions in the number of mail and parcels services worked by the Class 71s. The 09.57 Margate to Bricklayers Arms and the 18.35 Margate to Cannon Street were two of the workings still allocated to the Class 71s in this timetable. Their passenger workings were as previously the 'Night Ferry' and the 03.10 from Victoria to Ramsgate.

Meanwhile over on the South Western Division there were changes to the Class 74s' duties. The main change was to their morning duty, the 07.27 Southampton to Waterloo service. This was now worked by EMU stock rather than being locomotive hauled. The summer dated services from Waterloo to Weymouth Quay left at 09.55 in the morning and 20.30 in the evening. The morning departure ran daily until 4 October, resuming again on 28 April 1975. The evening working from Waterloo ran between July and September on Mondays, Wednesdays, and Fridays. At weekends the evening service left Waterloo slightly later at 20.37, running between 28 May and 21 September.

One of the original main requirements for the Class 74s had been to haul boat trains to and from Southampton and London. On 30 August, no fewer than six of these were run that day to Waterloo. Four were Class 74 hauled using Nos 74001, 74002, 74007, and 74009 which meant that all of the conditional trains in this timetable were run that day.

Overhauls of the Class 71s and 74s continued at Eastleigh. No 71001 was overhauled there during July and August 1974 at the same time as No 74005 which was also receiving attention.

Another Class 71 hauled freight derailed on 1 October 1974. The 22.23 Tonbridge to Chatham, consisting of No 71005 and 25 16T mineral wagons full of gypsum, derailed whilst passing through Halling station. The investigation found that the leading wheels of the first, second, and seventh wagons derailed over the Up line cess rail at 35 miles 423 yards. This was about halfway through the platform at Halling. The right-hand leading wheel of the last wagon also derailed, but at a point about nine yards before the point where the others had come off.

The consequent damage was considerable. The platform edging stones were damaged and the derailed wheelsets split the timber sleepers leading to multiple derailments into the 'four foot'. The train also divided at several points including

The number panel from No 71008 showing the TOPS number with traces of the previous number underneath. Below the number was the locomotive data panel. When renumbered in 1974 numbers were only placed by the driver's side. *Richard Vitler*

Above: **A slightly unusual picture of No 74001 at Bournemouth with a 4TC unit. The train formation seems too short for the usual 4REP and two 4TC formation.** *Class 47 Preservation Project Archive*

Left: **Complete with brake tender, No 74007 passes through Kensington Olympia on 20 May 1974 operating diesel power with a freight service from the Southern Region.** *Class 47 Preservation Project Archive*

No 74003 waiting to work the up Channel Islands boat train on Saturday 27 July 1974. When renumbered the new number was only applied on the driver's side. The previous number on the assistant's side has been painted out as seen here. *Grahame Arnold*

between the locomotive and the first wagon, and between the first and second wagons. The track damage was not rectified, and the line handed back for use, until 4 October.

Flange marks from the derailed wheelsets indicated a flange-climbing derailment. The train's speed at the point of derailment was between 35 and 40mph, confirmed by the 330 yards stopping distance of the derailed train under an emergency brake application. The only cause that could be identified was a cyclic track misalignment condition of some description.

No 71001 was used on departmental duties on 24 October. That morning it was seen propelling an inspection saloon into Dartford station.

The newspaper and mail train work of both the Class 71s and Class 74s was the subject of a *Railway Magazine* article published in December 1974. It was an aspect of their operations not often studied. In the piece Michael Oakley travelled firstly on the 03.00 Victoria to Ramsgate service; the train locomotive that morning was No 71002, its train comprising of 11 vehicles weighing 250 tons. Whilst the overall journey time was not especially fast, 2 hours 40 minutes, the train's 11 stops to unload newspapers and people could easily account for an hour of that time. The

No 74006, operating on diesel power, heads an empty stock train between Waterloo and Clapham Junction on 7 December 1974. This locomotive suffered major fire damage in November 1975 and remained out of service until its withdrawal in July 1976. *Class 47 Preservation Project Archive*

train was divided at Faversham, with seven vehicles going on to Ramsgate, the other four, also diagrammed for a Class 71, went to Dover. The journey time on this particular occasion was 117 minutes 38 seconds, this after a 14-minute late departure from Victoria. Some credible speeds were achieved during the journey, with 76mph recorded between Sittingbourne and Faversham, 79mph between Faversham and Whitstable, and on the 1 in 80/100 incline heading out of Margate 75mph was achieved. These speeds are particularly convincing given the short distances between station stops after the train left its first stop of Rochester. The Herne Bay to Birchington section is a little over four miles, but No 71002 was still able to touch 77mph in that time. The class's excellent acceleration was being used to good effect.

An unidentified Class 74 heads west at Wimbledon complete with a coal train from Acton which includes two brake tenders. The coal concentration depot at Tolworth is the most likely destination. In their later years the Class 74s were used regularly on this work. *Class 47 Preservation Project Archive*

The first of the class, No 74001 awaits departure from Waterloo with the 19.00 weekday Staines and Richmond vans train if the 18 headcode is correct.
Class 47 Preservation Project Archive

The second part of the article had a description of a run of the 02.45 Waterloo to Bournemouth hauled by No E6109. The train, a regular Class 74 duty for some years, comprised 10 vehicles weighing 340 tons. At Eastleigh four vehicles were removed bringing the train weight down to 200 tons. A further two vehicles were dropped off at Southampton, leaving just four vehicles weighing 135 tons to go forwards to Bournemouth. Some high speed running was recorded that morning with Walton-on-Thames passed at 91mph as was Weybridge. The highlight of the journey was the section between Basingstoke and Winchester. Worting Junction was passed at 74mph with the speed continuing to increase, Litchfield West was passed at 91mph, Micheldever at 94mph, and Wallers Ash East at 97mph. The stop at Winchester, 18¾ miles from Basingstoke, was reached in 15½ minutes.

Even with declining work for the Class 71s at this time, there were occasions when they were unable to fulfil their booked duties. The 12.00 Snowdown Colliery to Acton coal train was a regular booked Class 71 working, but on 13 January 1975, no member of the class was available for the duty. As a consequence, Class 47 No 47177, based at Immingham at the time, had to run light engine from Hoo Junction to pick up the duty instead.

The enthronement of Rt Rev Dr Donald Coggan on 24 January 1975 as Archbishop of Canterbury saw No 71004 used on a special train from Victoria to Canterbury East for people attending the service at Canterbury Cathedral. The train left Victoria at 11.30am with No 71004 reported as being in immaculate condition.

The Southern Region was hit by a nationwide dispute involving Workshop Supervisors during the spring of 1975. The dispute badly affected Eastleigh and caused a shortage of useable rolling stock. In turn this led to some unusual train formations. One such was on 29 March when the 14.38 Weymouth to Waterloo service was worked by No 74007 and two 4TC units. The stock was due to return as the 17.46 Waterloo to Bournemouth train, but unfortunately, No 74007 failed before departure and the train had to be cancelled.

The joint Eastleigh works and depot Open Day was held on 20 April 1975, both Nos 74003 and 74005 were amongst the locomotives exhibited. Over in the works, No 71005 was undergoing what in all likelihood would be its last overhaul at Eastleigh before being withdrawn.

The May 1975 timetable saw the Class 71 non-freight duties little changed from the previous one. The 'Night Ferry' still had 'summer' and 'winter' departure times from Victoria, the early morning departure from Dover unchanged at 07.20. The locomotive to be used on the 03.10 Victoria to Ramsgate passenger, parcel and newspaper train would run light from Stewarts Lane with a Class 33; this train continued to divide at Faversham, and the portion to Dover Priory also remained a Class 71 duty. The Class 71 for the other early morning duty from

Victoria, the 02.55 Maidstone van train, ran light separately.

The timing of the morning Waterloo to Weymouth Quay service was changed in this timetable to be slightly earlier at 09.36. The service ran from May until October. The evening weekend train from Weymouth Quay, at 20.37, ran between May and September. Mostly, as with previous timetables, the changeover of locomotives was at Bournemouth, although in the case of the 15.30 from Weymouth Quay the changeover as had happened in previous years was at Eastleigh.

Class 74 No 74003 had a lucky escape on 5 June when the leading bogie derailed at Micheldever whilst working the 02.45 Waterloo to Bournemouth newspaper train. The locomotive was undamaged, though it was reported that two miles of track was badly damaged. Both lines were blocked and normal working did not resume fully until 7 June.

By 1975, many of the problems with the Class 74s had been overcome and it seemed as if eventually both their availability and reliability were improving. Their performance was unquestionably good and they were more than capable of high speed running. The 02.15 Waterloo to Weymouth newspaper train was always heavily loaded and the train was booked to run the 55 miles between Woking and Southampton in 49 minutes, an average speed of 67mph. Their boat train work saw them running between Waterloo and Southampton on the same timings as the 100-minute Bournemouth services.

Class 71 workings with one of the region's instruction vehicles were not uncommon. On 9 July No 71011 was seen at Ashford with Instruction Car No 70155, a vehicle often used on such duties with the Class 71s.

The burnt out remains of No 74006 dumped at Basingstoke soon after the fire that eventually led to its withdrawal. The scale of the damage is apparent with the roof destroyed completely. The driver that day, Jim Dodswell, managed to escape through the cab window. *Paul Watson*

The first cloud on the horizon for the future of the Class 74s appeared on 7 November 1975. No 74006 caught fire at Worting Junction whilst working the 18.10 parcels train from Weymouth to Waterloo. The locomotive was moved subsequently to Eastleigh for the damage to be assessed, but the necessary repair work was not undertaken and as a result it was left at Eastleigh depot pending a final decision. The same 18.10 Weymouth to Waterloo parcels train was in trouble again five days later on 12 November. This time it came to a stand between New Milton and Sway with No 74010 having suffered damage to its shoegear. Class 33 No 33033 was used to render assistance and move the train forwards to Brockenhurst.

As the year came to an end, the passengers on the 09.00 Waterloo to Exeter St David's service on 11 December had a difficult journey. Departure from Waterloo was 11 minutes late, due to a defect with the original train locomotive No 33027. The only locomotive available was No 74009. This took the train as far as Woking where it was removed and replaced by No 33102. This locomotive was not without its own difficulties and was found to have problems with its ETH supply. At Salisbury it too was removed, and replaced by No 33007.

Waterloo

74008 shunting vans outside Waterloo.
Grahame Arnold

74009 stabled in the sunshine at Waterloo before its next duty. This area was taken over in time by the platforms for the Eurostar trains.
Class 47 Preservation Project Archive

Waterloo

74001 awaits departure from Waterloo with an empty stock train.
Class 47 Preservation Project Archive

No 74002 dropping down to Waterloo prior to working a boat train 26 August 1976 *Grahame Arnold*

11
The Final Years and Withdrawal 1976-1977

The year 1976 was to be pivotal for both the Class 71s and Class 74s. For the Class 71s it would be their final year in service. Whilst the Class 74s would remain in traffic, the class member that was already out of service would be withdrawn with another example soon to be in a similar position with question marks as to its future.

As the year began, though, it was business almost as usual. The 'Night Ferry's regular departure and indeed arrival platform at Victoria was Platform 2 and any alteration from this was highly unusual, mainly because of HM Customs requirements. Engineering work had shut the whole South Eastern side of Victoria on 25 January 1976 with the result that the train left from Platform 17 over on the 'Brighton' side.

Overhauls of the Class 74s continued until late on in their lives. No 74004 for example was seen on test after an overhaul at Eastleigh on 3 April 1976.

The South Eastern Division timetable introduced on 20 April showed just how little work was now allocated to the Class 71s. Their regular early morning 03.10 Victoria to Ramsgate passenger, parcel and newspaper train was still booked for the class. Elsewhere though, there was now only a small amount of mail and parcels traffic for them, two services in the morning and afternoon between Margate and Tonbridge and the 02.30 Faversham to Margate. The 09.57 Margate to Bricklayers Arms parcels service which in happier times was Class 71 hauled throughout, now saw them only take the train as far as Folkestone. There a Class 33 would take over for the

Above: **Waiting to be uncoupled from the 'Night Ferry', No 71013 rests at the buffers on Platform 2 at London Victoria station. By now the Class 71s were in the twilight years and the 'Night Ferry' itself would not survive much past the demise of the class.**
Class 47 Preservation Project Archive

The Final Years and Withdrawal 1976-1977

No 74003 working the 12.15 Southampton–Waterloo 'Pleasure seeker' ADEX through Eastleigh, 16 May 1976. This working was probably a fill-in turn using a set of boat train stock that had worked down to Southampton earlier. It is doubtful that the 'pleasure seekers' needed the services of the two GUVs in the rake that day. *Grahame Arnold*

majority of the journey to London. On Saturdays the 23.43 Norwood to Dover freight service ran only when required rather than every Saturday.

On Sundays, this timetable saw almost no work for the Class 71 except the two 'Night Ferry' trains and its two morning relief services running when required from Dover. The Sunday parcels duty in the previous timetable, the 18.55 Dover Priory to Victoria was withdrawn.

There was no change to the timings of the summer dated Waterloo to Weymouth Quay services in this timetable. These trains again ran from May to October, the locomotive changeover taking place at Bournemouth. The number of conditional boat train services to and from Southampton Docks was unchanged. On weekdays this meant up to seven such services could be run if required, all booked for electro-diesel locomotives.

A very late modification, made to around half of the Class 74s, was the fitting of an additional cab ventilator. These were fitted to the outer windscreen pillars of the cabs. Some locomotives including Nos 74003 and 74007 were withdrawn without having been fitted.

The first Class 74 to be withdrawn was the fire-damaged No 74006 when it was condemned on 20 June 1976. It remained at Eastleigh depot until 20 October when it was taken to the works and stored there.

Late on in its service life, No 71003 found itself over on the South Western Division. On 21 June it was used on a series of test trains also involving a 4VEP unit and a 2HAP unit. Unfortunately the reason for, and results of, these tests have never been made public.

Passengers travelling on the 16.00 Weymouth Quay to Waterloo service on 1 July had to be de-trained at Winchester after a fire started in the cab of No 74007. In spite of serious oil fumes in his cab, the driver was able to move the locomotive to a point adjacent to the station car park so that the local fire brigade could attend to the fire. The driver at one point was overcome by these fumes in his cab and had to be treated by an ambulance crew. A local newspaper report a few days later gave the cause of the fire as 'hot grids' on the locomotive.

The Class 71s in their later years suffered from a shortage of work. Freight tonnage on the Southern Region had declined as the country went through a long period of economic turmoil and uncertainty. Visitors to the Ashford Chart Leacon open weekend held on 21 and 22 August were told that the class would be withdrawn shortly. On display at the event were Nos 71006, 71007, 71008, 71011, 71013, and 71014, almost proving the previous statement as this amounted to nearly half the entire class.

The 'Night Ferry', their main passenger duty, was worked by them until the end. On 26 August 1976, No 71010 was used on the train. By now though the formation had reduced to two four-wheeled baggage cars, four Wagon-Lits sleeping cars, two BR catering vehicles, and a BR brake. The 19-coach loadings of the early 1960s were long gone. Whilst the non-sleeping car business had continued to rise, leading to separate trains needing to be run, the sleeping car side had been in decline. This meant the whole 'Night Ferry' operation had become far more expensive to operate. Space availability on the ferries was becoming limited by the growth in ferry wagon traffic, hence the reduction over the years of the train's size. One consequence of this was that it brought the train within the capabilities of the Class 73s.

The whole of the Class 71 were placed into storage on 23 September 1976. Reports from the time suggest that Nos 71006, 71007, and 71008 had been stored at Ashford for much of the summer in any case. Having been placed into store, the CM&EE's department put No 71012 to use for a while at Gillingham as an instruction locomotive. Nos 71004, 71009, 71013, and 71014 were kept at Hither Green, with Nos 71003, 71010, and 71011 at the London end of Ashford station.

The Class 74s continued in service for just over another year. Their dual-power capability worked in their favour for the time being at least. On 12 October Nos 74004, 74007, and 74010 were noted as all being on shed at Eastleigh.

Sunday 6 February 1977 saw No 74005 used on a quite remarkable working when it was used on the 15.08 Waterloo to Waterloo 'roundabout' service. The stock used was that from the 10.10 Exeter St Davids to Waterloo service, Due to engineering work en route causing the train to be diverted, it had arrived at Waterloo the wrong way round. The train included a Buffet car and this remained open during the trip through south-west London. By all accounts it did brisk business. The following Sunday saw a repeat performance, only this time No 74003 was the locomotive used.

The withdrawn No 74006 which had been stored at Eastleigh for a number of months was moved. On 20 February it was seen at Airport Sidings, whilst the final arrangements for its disposal were made.

During the long hot summer of 1976, several Class 71s were taken out of use before the decision was made to store all 14. No 71007 was one of those affected and is seen in store that summer. *Class 47 Preservation Project Archive*

Right: Whilst the damage suffered by No 74002 appears in this picture to be minimal, it was serious enough for the locomotive to be withdrawn in July 1977. The locomotive is seen here at Eastleigh depot awaiting final disposal. *Class 47 Preservation Project Archive*

Below: No 71010 waiting to depart from Faversham with the Ramsgate portion of the 03.00 from Victoria on 31 August 1976, a regular duty for them at the time. The Dover portion was then usually worked forward by another Class 71 but on this occasion Class 73 No 73133 was used instead. The Class 71 had just a month left in service. *Grahame Arnold*

The Final Years and Withdrawal 1976-1977

No 74004 was the chosen locomotive again, this time for the RCTS sponsored 'Wessex Venturer' tour on 23 April 1977. This used 4TC units Nos 405 and 430 plus buffet car and went from Waterloo to Southampton East Docks where No 07001 was used to take the train onto the Western Docks.

The last 'Class 74' timetable came into effect on 2 May. Their main services such as the Southampton boat trains and the Weymouth Quay services were booked for them, as always, subject to availability. From Waterloo, depending on demand there could be three such trains run, with up to seven from Southampton. The Weymouth Quay train 'season' ran until 24 October for the Monday to Friday service.

The second Class 74 to be withdrawn was No 74002. It had suffered minor accident damage in 1976, but was never repaired. According to some sources involved this damage occurred at Stewarts Lane when it was driven under power into the concrete stop block at the end of a set of trap points. It was suggested the driver said he had been stopped outside the signal box and been chatting to the signalman. At the end of the conversation he opened up the controller without realising he had not got the road and hence ended up going into the concrete block.

The locomotive was stored at Eastleigh depot where it was used as a source of spare parts for the rest of the class. It was officially withdrawn on 4 June 1977. The surviving eight locomotives continued to be active though not always successfully. Four days after No 74002 was withdrawn, No 74009 failed at Surbiton whilst working the 11.16 Southampton Docks to Waterloo boat train service. It was rescued by No 33064 which took the train as far as Clapham Junction. There both locomotives were removed to be replaced by No 33010 which took the train on to Waterloo. No 74004 also suffered minor accident damage around this time. It was seen in June in service with damage to the bottom left-hand corner of the No 2 end cab. This damage was never repaired and it ran in this condition until December when it was withdrawn.

The first of the class to be withdrawn, No 74006, had by now been sold and Cohen's scrapyard at Kettering received the locomotive on 15 June 1977. It was cut up soon afterwards, as by 5 August only the cabs remained intact.

On 28 June No 74009 failed between Worting Junction and Steventon with the 20.17 Waterloo to Weymouth Quay service. The following day however, saw No 74004 coming to

The train crew pose for the photographer on 2 December 1976 prior to No 74004 leaving Waterloo with an empty stock train
Class 47 Preservation Project Archive

A somewhat patchwork No 74010 at Eastleigh depot on 18 December 1976 with the already withdrawn No 74002 in the background.
Class 47 Preservation Project Archive

the rescue of No 47107 which had failed whilst working the 11.00 Eastleigh to Garston freight service. The Class 74 was sent from Basingstoke to help.

The Southern Region 'Anniversaries' tour commemorating both the Bournemouth and Portsmouth direct electrification schemes was run on 10 July 1977. The final leg of the tour was from Bournemouth to Waterloo and hauled by No 74007. The locomotive was suitably spruced up for the occasion and could be recognised in its final months in traffic by its distinctive white painted buffers. Other locomotives used that day included Nos 73132, 47143, and Class 33s Nos 33017 and 33027.

The use of a Class 74 on the Waterloo 'roundabout' to turn stock happened for the third time on 11 September. The service from Waterloo was the same as the two previous occasions and the stock was that from an earlier Exeter St Davids to Waterloo train. This time the locomotive employed was No 74005. The fourth and last occasion this happened was on 2 October when No 74001 was the locomotive used.

In the meantime, the class continued to see use on a variety of boat train services. The Waterloo to Weymouth Quay boat train services were a regular turn in their last few months in service. No 74001 was used on one on 17 October for example. The use of the locomotives on these trains came to an end when the 'season' finished on 24 October. By the time these trains resumed in 1978, all the Class 74s had been withdrawn.

The locomotives though still were able to prove their worth at times. No 74003 was busy on 26 October when it was used as the traction unit for two 4TC units in place of a failed 4REP EMU. The locomotive was used on the 11.00 from Bournemouth to Waterloo and returned on 13.30 Waterloo to Weymouth service. It was taken off the train at Bournemouth and used to power the 14.38 Weymouth to Waterloo service forwards from Bournemouth. Its day finished with it taking three 4TC units back to Bournemouth as the 17.30 Waterloo to Weymouth.

Meanwhile on the South Eastern Division the Class 71s were withdrawn 'en-bloc' on the same date, 26 November 1977, this following their period of storage. They remained where they had been stored, until final arrangements for their disposal were made.

The surviving Class 74s though continued to be active during what was to be their final two months in service with No 74010 in use on a Southampton boat train service on 16 November. On two separate occasions in November, members of the class were also seen on the London Midland Region at Willesden Junction. Firstly, on 18 November it was No 74001, whilst three days later it was the turn of No 74005 to appear

New Year's Eve 1976, and the driver's assistant watches on as railway staff try to manoeuvre a car out of the path of No 74005 as it attempts to make its way through the docks at Southampton. *Class 47 Preservation Project Archive*

there. No 74010 was active at Andover on 28 November hauling an Army train from the base at Ludgershall on the old Midland & South Western Junction Railway (MSWJR) line. An unidentified member of the class was also seen at Egham on 1 December running light on the Up line. It returned soon after heading in the opposite direction with a train of car flat wagons. On 2 December both Nos 74001 and 74005 were seen on shed at Eastleigh depot.

No 74005 waiting to depart 'Kingston roundabout' on 15 February 1977 ,the 15.08 Waterloo–New Malden–Twickenham–Waterloo. *Grahame Arnold*

Above: **In its latter days in service No 74004 suffered minor collision damage as seen here, though unlike No 74002 it was not serious enough to warrant withdrawal and the locomotive was condemned along with the bulk of the class on 31 December 1977.** *Class 47 Preservation Project Archive*

Below: **The 02.45 newspaper train was a regular Class 74 working throughout their lives. No 74004 awaits departure from Waterloo with the service on 29 August 1977.** *Grahame Arnold*

No 74005 waiting to depart Waterloo in the sunshine with the 15.08 'Kingston roundabout' on 11 September 1977 *Grahame Arnold*

The Final Years and Withdrawal 1976-1977

The use of Class 74s on the Weymouth Quay boat trains came to an end in October 1977. A few weeks before the end on 13 September No 74005 heads past Pokesdown bound for Waterloo. *Class 47 Preservation Project Archive*

Unlike the Class 71s the Class 74s were accorded the honour of a farewell railtour. Organised by the Diesel & Electric Group and the Railway Pictorial Publications Railtour a trip was run on 3 December 1977 called appropriately enough the 'Class 74 Farewell'. The route took in most of their old haunts and set out from Waterloo with No 74003, which had been active on a parcels train in the early hours, heading two 4TC units, Nos 412 and 424. Not surprisingly for the Class 74s, the tour was not without incident. On the way out from London the trip had been booked to run via East Putney but had to be diverted because the Guard had been left behind at Waterloo (he travelled on the 08.26 Hampton Court service).

No 74003 was used from Waterloo to Southampton Docks West, Southampton Liner Terminal to Romsey, Romsey to Lymington Pier, and Lymington Pier to Bournemouth via Brockenhurst. The locomotive had problems at Romsey when running on diesel as it ran hot and overheated, taking several attempts to re-start. Class 33 diesel No 33013, which was working a stone train, was used to assist in restarting No 74003's engine before the tour could continue towards Chandler's Ford. The tour was then held at Romsey for over an hour, likely to allow the engine to cool down. For the journey back to Waterloo from Bournemouth No 74010 was used. On the way home, the tour was routed via East Putney so as to compensate for missing it out in the morning. The same day as the farewell tour, No 74004 was active on a parcels duty.

On 4 December No 74004 was at work in the Basingstoke area, whilst No 74003, clearly recovered from its problems the previous day, was seen heading an Up freight service through Basingstoke station. The following Saturday, 10 December, No 74005 was noted hauling Waterloo & City line coach No S61S away from Waterloo, heading for repairs at Selhurst. A power failure on 16 December meant that No 74005 and a 4TC unit were used to work the shuttle service between Staines and Weybridge.

The end for the Class 74s came on 31 December 1977, when the remaining eight locomotives were withdrawn. They were stored at various locations until their final sale and disposal could be arranged.

Disposal

The 24 locomotives that made up the Class 71 and Class 74 were disposed of at a number of different locations. No 71001 was claimed by the NRM for the National Collection, with the other 23 locomotives all sent for scrap.

Nos 71001, 71002, 71003, 71005, 71006, 71007, 71008, 71010, 71011, and 71012 had been stored at several locations around Ashford, with the other four locomotives stored at Hither Green. The scrapping of the Class 71s was carried at two locations: BREL Doncaster or J. Cashmore Ltd in Newport in south Wales.

Above: **In its last months in service, No 74007** was always recognisable with its silver painted buffers. In this view dated 5 November 1977, the locomotive is seen at the entrance to Wimbledon EMU depot with two 4SUB units stabled in the background.
Class 47 Preservation Project Archive

Left: In pale winter sunshine, **No 74004** runs around its train at Southampton Docks during the final weeks of Class 74 operations.
Class 47 Preservation Project Archive

The first locomotives to go for scrap were Nos 71002, 71005, 71006, 71007, 71008, and 71012, which went to J. Cashmore Ltd in August 1978. Several including Nos 71005, 71006 and 71012 were kept at Old Oak Common from 20 August to 27 August whilst en route to Wales. They had been moved from Ashford to Stewarts Lane on 18 August along with Nos 71002 and 71007. The latter on its journey to Newport spent almost a month parked up at Swindon works before arriving at Cashmore's on 23 September. No 71003 however remained at Ashford and was displayed at the Open Weekend at Chart Leacon on 19 and 20 August 1978.

The Final Years and Withdrawal 1976-1977

Almost the end. Nos 71009 and 71014 arrive at Doncaster on 9 August 1979 for scrapping towed by Class 31 No 31253.
Barrie Watkins/Class 47 Preservation Project Archive

In the meantime there were some accounting and other processes British Rail had to complete with regard to the withdrawn locomotives. Each year the Investment Committee would formally agree to the withdrawal of locomotives from the previous year with the reasons why. The memorandum to the committee dated September 1978 covering both the Class 71s and 74s' withdrawal makes interesting reading. It said that BR's policy was for the elimination and small non-standard classes and that the withdrawal of electric locomotives in 1977 was 'not well forecast'. The main reason being that it had not been anticipated that the Southern Region would reach the conclusion in 1977 that their Class 71 (14 locomotives) and Class 74 (nine locomotives) would no longer be required.

Nos 71004, 71009, 71010, 71011, 71013 and 71014, were towed from Stewarts Lane to Temple Mills Yard at Stratford on 21 and 22 June 1979 before being moved in groups to BREL Doncaster between 20 and 23 July. Whilst at Temple Mills, No 71014 was seen sporting the headboard from the Railway Pictorial Publications Railtours 'Southern Invader' railtour that was run on 7 April. Much of No 71011 had been cut up by early November 1979. This meant just one locomotive was still at Stewart's Lane; No 71003. It left there on 21 January 1980 for March, before being moved on to Doncaster. It was seen at Doncaster intact on 17 Feb, but was scrapped very soon afterwards.

The Class 74s were withdrawn at the same time, bar the two damaged examples. A number were stored at Eastleigh, with Nos 74003, 74005 and 74009 on display at the works Open Day held on 30 April 1978. Several companies and locations were involved in their disposal. Bird's based at Long Marston in Warwickshire bought five of them, and Nos 74001, 74004, 74007, 74008, and 74009 were moved to their yard on 9 August 1978. Scrapping of these locomotives began very soon after their arrival. Work was well underway for example on No 74009 by 29 October.

The last of the class to be broken up was No 71003, appropriately enough at Doncaster where it had been built 20 years earlier. Here in this late February 1980 view, whilst much of the electrical equipment has been removed, the locomotive's bodywork is still intact, though not for much longer.
Class 47 Preservation Project Archive

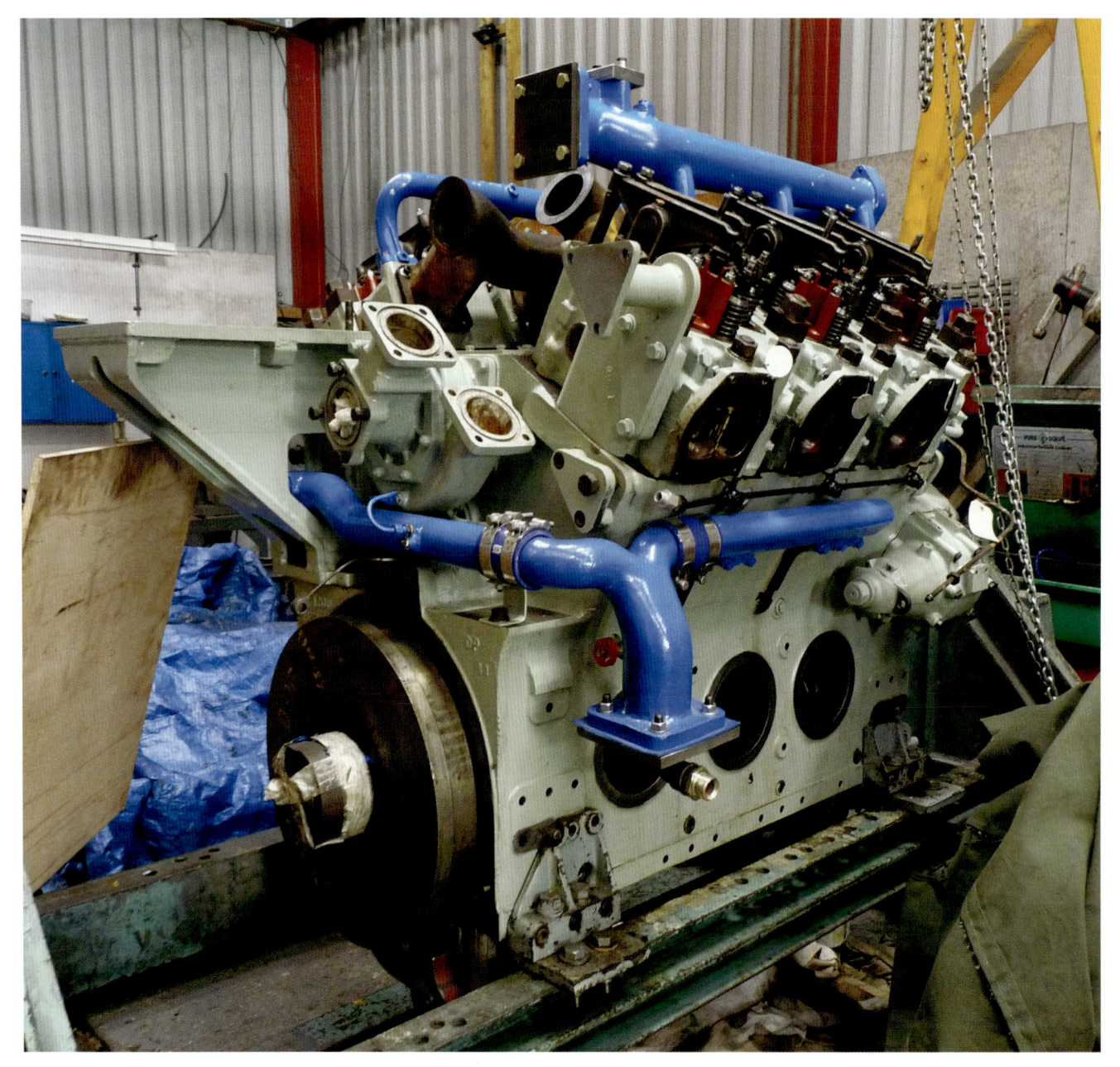

Perhaps the only surviving piece of Class 74 is this Paxman engine retrieved from No 74009. This picture taken on 12 June 2016 shows it being reconditioned at Williton, on the West Somerset Railway ready for use in Class 14 No D9526. *B. Pizer*

J. Cashmore Ltd bought Nos 74002 and 74003. No 74002 was taken there on 8 December 1977, but No 74003 did not arrive there until three years later. Pounds Shipowners & Shipbreakers Ltd in Portsmouth acquired No 74005, but a lack of rail access to their site meant the locomotive was broken up by their staff at BR's Fratton depot having been moved there on 9 December 1980.

For a while it had been thought that No 74010 would be taken into Departmental stock. In August 1978 it was moved from Eastleigh to Derby via Clapham Junction for use as a mobile generator. Whilst at Clapham, it was observed with 'we will miss you 74' chalked on the rubbing plate at one end of the locomotive. The plan for it to be used as a departmental locomotive was not taken further and in December 1978 No 74010 was noted in store at Derby Etches Park. There it remained until it left Derby for Doncaster in the company of No 24063 which was also going for scrap and No RDB968007 (formerly No 24061) which was going for repair. The trio arrived at Doncaster on 4 July 1979. Scrapping of No 74010 was completed by October that year. [pic P1060860 hereabouts]

One part of one Class 74 does has survived, the Paxman engine that was in No 74009 when it was scrapped. When purchased by its current owners part of the Class 74 bedplate was still attached at the bottom. As this book went to print, this engine was being installed in the preserved Class 14 No D9526. It has been fully overhauled after a long period of storage with a marine salvager in Glasgow.

The Farewell Tour

Above: **The tour enabled passengers to enjoy one of the last occasions a Class 74 crossed Canute Road as the tour left Southampton Docks. Railway staff are on hand to hold up the traffic. At the front of the queue is a Mark 1 Ford Cortina, with a Mark 3 Cortina behind.** *Class 47 Preservation Project Archive*

Below: **One of the tour's photographic stops was at Northam. In the background we see one passenger clambering back inside the 4TC.**
Class 47 Preservation Project Archive

The Class 74s were given a farewell railtour, sponsored by the DEG and RPPR. No 74003 was the motive power for much of the day. A sticker type headboard was provided at one end as seen here in this picture taken at Chandler's Ford. *Class 47 Preservation Project Archive*

12
Preservation

Unlike the three Southern Railway Co-Co electric locomotives before them, one of the Class 71 locomotives was saved for official preservation. After withdrawal in November 1977, No 71001 was stored at Ashford Chart Leacon depot until June 1978. It had been there since 4 October 1976 whilst awaiting a decision as to its future. It was moved with steam locomotive No 30777 *Sir Lamiel* on 23 June 1978, spending time stabled at Bromley South station before being towed north that night bound for Doncaster works. The locomotive was stabled at Doncaster depot on 3 July, before entering the works for restoration.

No 71001 remained at Doncaster for some eight months and was repainted in its original green livery with red and white lining. However, modifications made after the livery was modified were retained, such as the cab rain strips and the cab ventilators. It was outshopped on 13 March 1979 as No E5001 and moved by Class 40 No 40099 to the National Railway Museum four days later. It was put on display on 19 March. One oddity of the preserved No E5001 is that its No 1 end bogie has spoked wheels; whilst the No 2 end bogie has solid wheels.

It remained at the NRM until in 1988 it began to be made available for display at Open days and other such events. Its first appearance away from York was at Basingstoke on 24 and 25 September 1988 organised by the Salisbury Area Manager, Gerald Daniels. This was followed by attendance at Waterloo on 1 October for the Ian Allan/Network SouthEast Day and at Bescot Open Day eight days after that, before returning to the NRM. Appropriately its next journey was to Ashford for the Ashford 150 celebrations.

Thoughts then turned to the possibility of the locomotive returning to active use and again No E5001 made the journey from York to Ashford Chart Leacon on 14 May 1992 to be brought back to working order. During this work, No E5001 was displayed at the Ashford Chart Leacon Open Day on Saturday 6 June.

Above: **No 71001 and 30777 were parked at Bromley South temporarily whilst en route to Doncaster in June 1978. In time, of course, both locomotives would return to duty on the mainline.** *Class 47 Preservation Project Archive*

No 71001 spent nine months at Doncaster being restored to almost original condition. Here the locomotive is seen in the paint shop being prepared for painting in its original lined green livery once again.
Class 47 Preservation Project Archive

The restoration work took three months to complete and No E5001 hauled a successful test train from Ashford to Dover Western Docks and back on 28 August. Nine days later it was used on a Network SouthEast staff special 'The Network Arrow' when it hauled 4CEP units Nos 1559 and 1594 from Ashford to Victoria and return. Originally, the return journey had been intended to reach Dover Western Docks, but a booster set fault meant the train was terminated early at Ashford.

The first public railtours using No E5001 were run on 12 and 13 September between Waterloo and Bournemouth and return in connection with the Open Day there. On the journey on 13 September, Class 73 No 73132, which had been provided as insurance on the rear of the train, failed when running round at Bournemouth. No E5001 by comparison, performed faultlessly on both days.

No E5001 was seen inside the confines of Ashford Level 5 depot on 24 April 1993.

It was next used on a railtour over the LSWR mainline on 17 July 1993, the 'DC Green Flasher'. On this occasion it was used on the leg between Waterloo and Southampton.

No E5001 was due to be retired to the St Leonards centre at Hastings after a final railtour on 25 March 1995, but unfortunately it failed at Eastleigh with flat batteries and circuit breaker problems whilst being prepared. Rail privatisation meant that the locomotive was stored out of use at Ashford Chart Leacon for much of 1995, though for some of the year it

After arrival at the National Railway Museum, No E5001 was put on display a few days later. *Class 47 Preservation Project Archive*

After nearly 10 years on display at the NRM in York, No E5001 was made available as an exhibit for open days such as the one at Bescot on 10 October 1988. In company with Class 77 No E27000 it is towed away from the event passing through Bescot station. *Class 47 Preservation Project Archive*

was kept at Eastleigh. It returned to work on the mainline the following year when it was used on the 'Southern Coastman' from Basingstoke on 20 April. A few days after the tour the locomotive was taken north to be an exhibit at the Open Day held at Crewe Electric depot on 3 May 1997.

It relocated to St Leonard's depot near Hastings in November 1997, remaining there until 2000 when it was moved to Crewe works and then onto the carriage Sheds at Crewe. It stayed at Crewe for a year before being moved to the more familiar territory of Stewarts Lane in April 2001.

The Open Day at Doncaster works held on 27 July 2003 saw the locomotive return to its birthplace for the first time since its restoration was completed in 1979. In 2010 it was again on familiar territory as an exhibit at Ashford Chart Leacon.

The locomotive spent some time on display at the NRM's outstation at Shildon before being moved again, this time to Barrow Hill roundhouse near Chesterfield. Whilst its external condition has deteriorated after a period stored outside, the locomotive is mechanically and electrically complete. The beginning of 2017 saw the locomotive back at Locomotion in Shildon. It is understood that a repaint is planned, and for the next phase of its preserved life, the locomotive will be in BR blue as No 71001 once again.

No E5001's return to mainline operations was on 12 September 1992 when it was used on the 'Royal Wessex' railtour from Waterloo to Bournemouth. The train with No 73132 and two 4TC units in tow passes Lyndhurst Road. *Class 47 Preservation Project Archive*

Conclusion

The booster system of controlling DC locomotives was unique to the Southern Railway/Region's third-rail network. The need for this system arose because it was, and indeed almost certainly still is, the only third rail system running electrically-hauled heavy freight trains. These in the era of loose-coupled freight wagons, required the locomotive to maintain some tractive effort across gaps in the third-rail power supply.

Alfred Raworth developed the idea in the 1930s, which then became the three Co-Co mixed traffic locomotives. These machines proved the practicality of using booster control and also demonstrated the need to protect the locomotives from short circuits and fluctuating voltages in the third rails. The Branchu current limiter device and various other protection relays were developed on these machines. A matter of future importance nationally, was the development of the DSD (Driver Safety Device) and safe braking arrangements for unfitted freight trains which allowed for the single manning of freight trains, as and when union agreement was forthcoming.

These three locomotives had some electrical weaknesses, that could have been designed out had a production batch had been built. They were nevertheless reliable and useful locomotives, capable of hauling any freight train then running on the Southern Railway and could match the performance of the Portsmouth direct line express 4COR EMUs in passenger service. By the 1960s their 75mph maximum speed and lack of train air brakes reduced their usefulness. However, their steam heat boilers meant they were retained until the end of that need on the Southern Region finally made them surplus to requirements.

The post-war era brought the need for the more powerful but lighter 90mph Bo-Bo Class 71 locomotives rather than the heavy 75mph Co-Co basically freight Class 70 locomotives of earlier times. From a performance point of view, the new design could achieve a peak drawbar power of 3,800hp at 47mph, and outperform a Class 55 'Deltic' diesel locomotive up to a speed of 67mph. This enhanced performance brought to the fore the problems of wheelslip, to which the booster electrical circuit arrangement was particularly susceptible. Development work to control wheelslip pointed the way towards very fast acting electronic control of the booster set.

Reduction in freight train working and an increasing use of multiple unit trains for passenger traffic helped bring about their end. No E5001 is the only survivor as a museum exhibit.

The Bournemouth electrification scheme required push-pull fitted electric locomotives fitted with small diesel engines, for the Southampton Docks traffic. As a result, 10 of the Class 71 electric locomotives were converted to become the Class 74 electro-diesels. The conversion work included the electronic booster control system developed using Class 71 No E5013. The high mechanical inertia and low electrical inertia of the booster sets could produce very large electrical surges which were damaging to the equipment. The electro-mechanical protection devices fitted to the existing locomotives were not fast enough acting to cope. To counter this problem, use was made of fast-acting electronic control of the booster generator fields in the converted locomotives.

Unfortunately, history has shown that the rail industry in 1967 had yet to learn how to use electronic systems in a traction environment. The concept was the right one, but the application was too early. Several more years of development both of the electronic components and satisfactory installation techniques would be required before solid state control systems would become routine, something Mr Hawes alluded to in his 1975 paper on the class. Meanwhile, it took about five years of work before the Class 74s could be regarded as useful and fairly reliable machines.

Their other major technical problem was that the Paxman diesel engine did not cope well with the typical stop start short time running at full power then shut down cycle that was the daily lot of an electro-diesel locomotive's engine. Many years development work by engine manufacturers would have to take place before the problems of rapid thermal load cycling of fast running diesel engines were understood and ultimately overcome.

With a justifiable reputation for unreliability and a loss of the traffic they were built for, it is understandable that their superb performance when they did work as intended could not save them from withdrawal and the scrapyard. At that time the rugged and far more reliable Class 73 electro-diesels could do what work was left, supplemented by the region's Class 33 diesel locomotives.

Will we see any more booster locomotives built in the future? The answer to that has to be no. This is because the DC series wound traction motor has been largely replaced by the variable frequency three phase AC traction motor and its solid state inverter controls.

Future electric freight locomotive requirements are likely to be driven by the needs of the intermodal container traffic to utilise the electrified network and accelerate freight trains. This would suggest an electro-diesel updated version of the Class 92 electric locomotive. DC third rail capability of such machines, as well as 25kv AC, could apply to locomotives serving both the Southampton Docks and Dollands Moor traffic flows. If it was felt desirable to have a facility to maintain tractive effort across gaps in the third rail, or indeed through neutral sections of overhead 25kv lines, then possibly a motor driven flywheel could provide the energy reserve. Far more likely though would be the use of alternative modern technology such as super capacitors.

Whatever comes to fruition will be totally different to the development story of the Classes 70 (the original and genuine electric locomotives), 71 and 74 as told here and in *Southern Way Special Issue No11*.

Appendix 1
Locomotive History

CLASS 71

Pre TOPS Nos	TOPS No.	To Stock	Withdrawn	Scrapped	Disposal
E5000/E5024	–	24/12/1958	–	–	Converted to Class 74
E5001	71001	31/01/1959	26/11/1977	–	Preserved NRM
E5002	71002	24/02/1959	26/11/1977	01/79	J. Cashmore Ltd Newport
E5003	–	20/03/1959	–	–	Converted to Class 74
E5004	71004	16/04/1959	26/11/1977	01/80	BREL Doncaster
E5005	–	12/05/1959	–	–	Converted to Class 74
E5006	–	02/06/1959	–	–	Converted to Class 74
E5007	71007	19/06/1959	26/11/1977	11/78	J. Cashmore Ltd Newport
E5008	71008	17/07/1959	26/11/1977	10/78	J. Cashmore Ltd Newport
E5009	71009	08/08/1959	26/11/1977	09/79	BREL Doncaster
E5010	71010	04/09/1959	26/11/1977	08/79	BREL Doncaster
E5011	71011	30/09/1959	26/11/1977	12/79	BREL Doncaster
E5012	71012	27/10/1959	26/11/1977	10/78	J. Cashmore Ltd Newport
E5013	71013	08/12/1959	26/11/1977	11/79	BREL Doncaster
E5014	71014	20/02/1960	26/11/1977	09/79	BREL Doncaster
E5015	–	20/02/1960	–	–	Converted to Class 74
E5016	–	05/04/1960	–	–	Converted to Class 74
E5017	–	24/03/1960	–	–	Converted to Class 74
E5018/E5003	71003	27/04/1960	26/11/1977	03/80	BREL Doncaster
E5019	–	17/05/1960	–	–	Converted to Class 74
E5020/E5005	71005	15/06/1960	26/11/1977	11/78	J. Cashmore Ltd Newport
E5021	–	27/07/1960	–	–	Converted to Class 74
E5022/E5006	71006	31/08/1960	26/11/1977	10/78	J. Cashmore Ltd Newport
E5023	–	25/10/1960	–	–	Converted to Class 74

CLASS 74

Pre TOPS Nos	TOPS No.	To Stock	Withdrawn	Scrapped	Disposal
E6101/E5015	74001	11/02/1968	12/77	08/78	Birds Ltd Long Marston
E6102/E5016	74002	05/11/1967	06/77	12/77	J. Cashmore Ltd Newport
E6103/E5006	74003	10/12/1967	12/77	12/80	J. Cashmore Ltd Newport
E6104/E5024	74004	25/02/1968	12/77	08/78	Birds Ltd Long Marston
E6105/E5019	74005	10/03/1968	12/77	01/81	Pounds Ltd at Fratton
E6106/E5023	74006	17/03/1968	06/76	06/77	G. Cohen Ltd Kettering
E6107/E5003	74007	31/03/1968	12/77	08/78	Birds Ltd Long Marston
E6108/E5005	74008	07/04/1968	12/77	08/78	Birds Ltd Long Marston
E6109/E5017	74009	28/04/1968	12/77	08/78	Birds Ltd Long Marston
E6110/E5021	74010	09/06/1968	12/77	10/79	BREL Doncaster

Appendix 2
Main technical Dimensions

	Class 71	Class 74
Length	50ft 7in	50ft 5¾in
Height	13ft 1in	13ft 1in
Width	9ft 3 1/16in	9ft 3 1/16in
Wheel Diameter	4ft 0in	4ft 0in
Bogie Wheelbase	10ft 6in	10ft 6in
Bogie Centres	27ft 0in	27ft 0in
Total Wheelbase	37ft 6in	37ft 6in
Traction Motor Type	EE Type EE532A	EE Type EE532A or EE532 BR1
Traction Motor 1 hour rating	638hp	638hp
Total 1 hour rating	2552hp	2552hp
Gear Ratio	76:22	76:22
Tractive Effort	45,000lb	Diesel: 40,000lb Electric: 47,500lb
One Hour Tractive Effort	20000lb at 47mph	Diesel: 18,100lb at 65mph Electric: 12,400lb at 69.6mph
Continuous Tractive Effort	12400lb at 69.6mph	18200lb at 48mph
Maximum Speed	90mph	90mph
Weight	77 tons	84 tons 16cwt
Route Availability	6	7
Vacuum Exhausters	Reavell FRU 5¼ x 10in	Reavell FRU 5¼ x 10in
Control Voltage	45-110 volts	45-110 volts
Auxiliary Generator	EE910	–
Auxiliary M-G Rating	9.2kw, 83.5A, 110v	–
Booster Generator	EE836A or 1B	EE836/2D
Booster Generator Rating	1080kw 1600A 675v at 1750rpm	1080kw 1600A 675v at 1750rpm
Alternator	–	EE 910/2C
Battery Type	Nife ES8 110v	DP RSKA 77M/4 77 AH
Air Compressor Type	Westinghouse DHC3	Westinghouse DHC3
Air Compressor Capacity	48cu ft/min 15.5A 675v	48cu ft/min 15.5A 675v
Engine	–	Paxman 6YJXL
Engine Output	–	650hp at 1500rpm
Fuel Tank Capacity	–	310 gallons
Main Generator	–	EE843/B or EE843/C
Main Alternator	–	EE910/2C
Control Alternator	–	Newton M423

Bibliography

Primary Sources – Books
Boocock, C. – *Railway Liveries: BR Traction 1948-1995*
Brown, D. – *Southern Electric Volume 2*
Cooper, B. K. – *Electric Trains in Britain*
Glover, J. – *Southern Electric*
Haresnape, B. – *British Rail Fleet Survey No 6 Electric Locomotives*
Lilley, S., Hiscock, J. G., Ward, R – *Class 47: 50 Years of Locomotive History*
Lilley, S., and Wenyon, J. – *Southern Way Special Issue 11 The 'Booster' Locos CC1/CC2/20003.*
Marsden, C. J. – *DC Electrics*
Morgan, J. C. – *Southern EMUs*
Moody, G. T. – *Southern Electric 1909-1979*
Pallant, N., and Bird, D. – *BR Locomotives: 1 Diesel & Electric Locomotives of the Southern Region.*
Rayner, B. – *Southern Electrics A Pictorial Survey*
Southern Way Special Issue: Southern Way Special No 12: A Third-Rail Centenary

Primary Sources – Magazines
LCGB Bulletin
Railway Magazine
Railway Observer
Railways South East
Railway World

Primary Sources – Reports
British Transport Commission – *Modernisation and Re-Equipment of British Railways* December 1954
Raworth, A. – *Report on Proposed Extensions of Electrification May 1944 Southern Railway.*

Other Sources
The papers of A. T. H Tayler CEng, FIMechE

Primary Sources – Technical Papers
Allen, R. J. – *Technical Memorandum TM FM C52TS Monobloc Wheels: BR Service Experience to Date – October 1973*
Allen, R. J. – *Technical Memorandum TM FM 40 C52TS Wheels Second Interim Report – March 1974*
Hawes, A. – *Class 74 electro-diesel locomotives of British Rail Southern Region, with particular reference to the control system – 30/04/1975*
Kibblewhite, G. G. – *British Railways Experience with Electronic Control Gear on Locomotives: 1966/68–1969*
Lucas, H. W. and Wojtas, B. – *Automatic Wheelslip Control – 14/11/1966*
McLoughlin, M. and Green, D. J. – *Technical Memorandum TM FM 49 Derailment of 6T80 22:23 Tonbridge to Chatham at Halling 01/10/1974 – December 1974*
Report E319D Stresses in Rail Ends –1962
Sykes, W. J. A. – *The Bournemouth Electrification – 16/12/1968*
Sykes, W. J. A. – *Southern Region Electrification – 18/06/1962*

Index

20001 ....23, 28, 70
20002 ....23, 28, 31, 70
20003..5, 6, 21, 25, 28

Accidents 33, 36, 38, 83, 87
Ashford, F. 56, 57
Ashford 5, 7, 30, 31, 32, 33, 35, 36, 37,
38, 41, 44, 49, 53, 69, 82, 84, 85, 87,
88, 93, 97, 103, 104, 109, 110, 111
Availability targets 34, 36, 37, 39, 40, 69,
74, 75, 77, 82, 93

Barman, Christian................................8, 19, 20
Batteries 18, 65, 79, 110
Battersea Wharf 26, 30
Black, Misha...............................8, 9, 10, 18, 19, 20, 42
Bloomfield, J. 19, 20, 66
Boiler 6, 8, 112
Bond, R. C. 8, 19, 23
Booster locomotive 5, 6, 25, 32, 51, 53,
54, 70, 112
'Bournemouth Belle' 36

Bournemouth electrification........29, 33, 36,
50, 52, 52, 55, 57, 74, 112
BR Board 54, 57, 58, 59, 61, 66, 69
BR/Sulzer Type 2 32, 53
BRCW Type 28, 32, 33, 34, 35, 36,
53, 57, 64
Brighton 6, 8, 9, 10, 18, 21, 23, 28, 30,
34, 36, 49, 56, 58, 59, 60, 61,
62, 66, 87, 96
Brown-Boveri 12
Brunswick Green 19
Brush Type 4 ....43, 56, 57, 61, 69
Bulleid, O. V. S. 6

Cabside...20, 32
Carriage green 19, 20, 43
Cashmore, J. 103, 104, 106, 113
Casualty rate 34
CC4 6
Central Division.....23, 24, 27, 31, 32, 34, 39,
55, 85, 87
Chart Leacon........36, 97, 104, 109, 110, 111
Co-Co...6, 31
Cock, C. M. 6
Cohen's...99, 113
Collision..78, 83, 87
Continuous rating...13
Cook, K. J. 10, 19
Cox, E. S. 19, 20
Crewe........32, 36, 37, 38, 43, 49, 54, 59, 60,
61, 62, 63, 64, 66, 68, 69, 70,
75, 77, 78, 83, 111

'Deltic' 13
Departmental stock................................106

Design Panel 9, 18, 19, 20, 43
Diagrams 37, 39, 57, 77
Diesel Traction......................................5, 35
Doncaster........6, 8, 9, 10, 11, 20, 22, 23, 24,
26, 30, 42, 103, 105,
106, 109, 111
Driver training..............10, 21, 22, 23, 24, 25
Durnsford Road 21, 69

Eastern Region............10, 19, 23, 24, 25, 61
Electrification Committee.....8, 9, 10, 21, 23,
24, 25, 26, 28, 30, 59
Elliott, John 6
English Electric............6, 9, 11, 12, 13, 22, 23,
27, 35, 50, 56, 57, 58, 59, 60, 61, 62,
62, 63, 64, 65, 68, 69, 75, 79

Fitch S. A..10, 24
Flashover 50, 51, 52
French 8, 30, 85, 86

Glass Reinforced Plastic................56, 57, 63
'Golden Arrow' 7, 25, 28, 31, 32, 33, 34,
35, 36, 37, 38, 39, 40, 41,
49, 82, 83, 84, 85, 86
Gomersal, H. R. 59

HA 6, 12, 13, 20, 23, 24, 25, 28, 30, 31,
32, 34, 35, 36, 37, 38, 43, 44,
53, 55, 58, 59, 61
Harrison, J. F. 20, 35, 44, 57, 58, 66
HB 12, 59, 63, 64, 67, 68, 69, 70
Headcode 9, 48, 49, 72
Hoff, R. B. 58
Hopkins, C. P. 7, 10, 20, 28, 55

Ibbotson, L. W. 57
Ilston, R. B. 7
Industrial Design Department 44, 57, 66
Institution of Locomotive Engineers ...31, 51

Jarvis, Ronald 8, 18, 19, 20, 44, 56, 57

Kent Coast 6, 7, 8, 22, 31, 32, 35, 55, 59
Kibblewhite, G. G. 74

LBSCR 5
Lightband, Dennis 13, 22
London Midland Region 25, 29, 54, 86, 100
Loudaphone 63
Louvres 9, 11, 20, 49
Lucas, H. W. 51
Lynes, Lionel...6

'Man of Kent' 31, 84
Maximum Tractive Effort....................13, 51
McKenna, David 18, 42, 58
Metropolitan-Vickers 29, 30

Missenden, Eustace 5

National Railway Museum 109, 111
National Traction Plan 36, 39
'Night Ferry' 7, 24, 25, 26, 27, 29, 30, 31,
32, 34, 35, 36, 37, 38, 39, 41,
42, 82, 84, 85, 86, 89, 92, 97
Nock, O. S. 26, 27, 29

Pantograph 11, 12, 13, 18
Pennsylvania 8
Phase One 10, 23, 24, 25
Phase Two....10, 22, 23, 24, 25, 28, 30, 32, 55
Pounds Shipowners & Shipbreakers 106
Pullman........7, 28, 31, 33, 35, 36, 49, 64, 86

Railtours...........36, 39, 70, 71, 72, 89, 103,
105, 107, 108, 110, 111
Railway Magazine 26, 29, 32, 34, 36, 56, 90
Railway Observer 54
Railway World................................35, 41
Raworth, Alfred 5, 6, 112
Robson, A. E. 43, 44, 60, 69
Rogers, J. F. 36
Royal Train 35

Secondman 66, 78
SKF 12
Skidding..52
Smart, S. W. 6
Smyth, H. S. 23
South Eastern Division......27, 28, 32, 35, 36,
37, 39, 40, 54, 57, 69, 82,
84, 96, 100
Southern Railway..........5, 12, 13, 14, 20, 39,
54, 70, 109, 112
Southern Region 6, 7, 8, 9, 10, 13, 18, 19,
20, 21, 22, 23, 26, 28, 30, 31, 33, 34, 35,
36, 39, 40, 50, 53, 55, 56, 57, 58, 59, 60,
61, 62, 64, 65, 66, 68, 69, 70, 72, 75, 86,
89, 92, 97, 100, 105, 112
Stewarts Lane 21, 22, 25, 27, 30, 31, 32,
33, 36, 68, 69, 78, 82, 92, 99,
104, 105, 111
Swift, H. H...6, 8, 19
Swiss Locomotive
Manufacturing Co Ltd.....................9, 11
Sykes, W. J. A................9, 10, 23, 24, 25, 42,
58, 60, 74

Warder, S. B. 7, 8, 34, 55, 57, 58
Weedon, Mr 21, 23, 25
Wheelslip tests 33, 49, 40, 51, 52, 65
Wheelspin..23, 51
Wilkes, E. G. M. 43
Williams, George 10, 18, 19, 20, 56, 57
Wojtas, B. 51
Work in Hand Report 57

The Southern Way
The regular volume for the Southern devotee

SPECIAL ISSUES

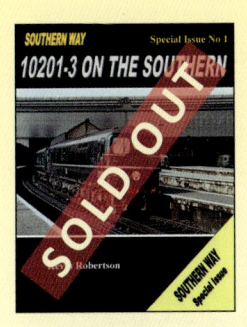

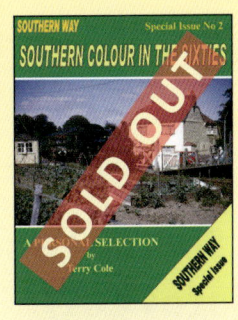

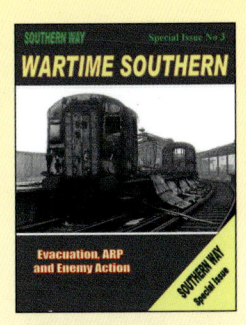

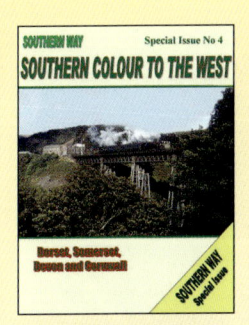

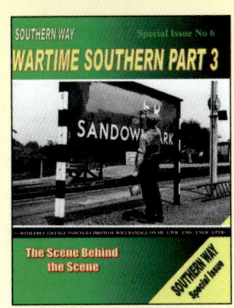

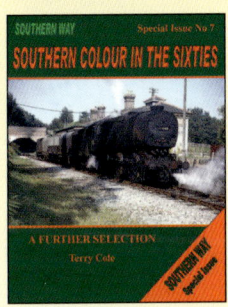

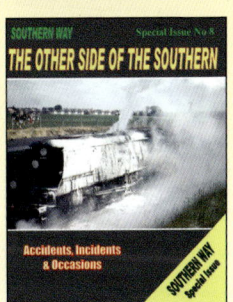

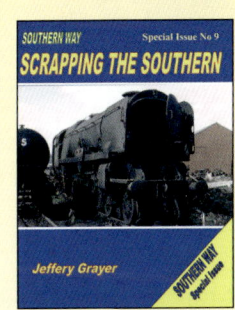

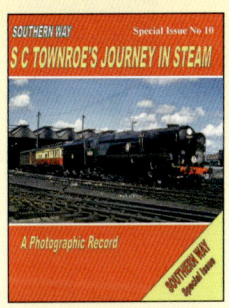

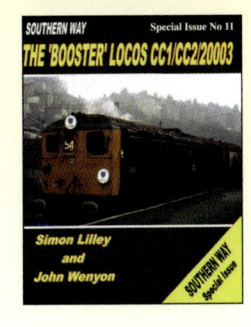

SOUTHERN WAY 'Special Issues'
Nos 3 to 5 £14.95. Nos 6 to 12 £16.50

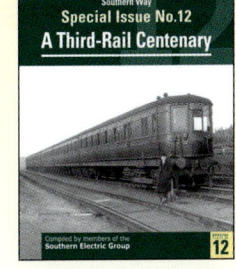

Editorial matters only to: editorial@thesouthernway.co.uk 01489 877880 or by post to:

The Southern Way (Kevin Robertson)
Conway, Warnford Rd, Corhampton
Hants SO32 3ND

Orders, subscriptions and sales enquiries to:
Crécy Publishing
1a Ringway Trading Est, Shadowmoss Rd,
Manchester M22 5LH

0161 499 0024
www.crecy.co.uk

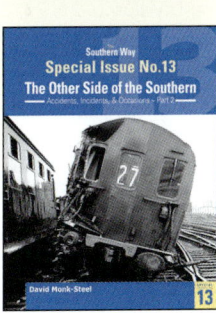

The Southern Way
SPECIAL ISSUE
The regular volume for the Southern devotee

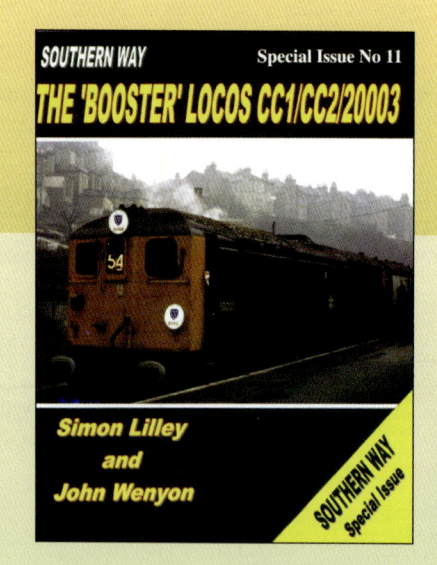

Southern Way Special Issue No 11
The 'Booster' locos CC1/CC2/2003
Simon Lilley and John Wenyon

An integral part of the Southern scene from the 1940s and 1950s, the three 'Booster' locomotives were the product of innovation by both the mechanical and electric departments of the SR.

Famed for both their reliability and flexibility in working, they were equally at home on long unfitted freight trains or fast express workings. Indeed such was their prowess that even late in their lives they were trusted with special, even Royal, duties.

The story of these engines has long been missing from the annals of railway history but this can now be put right with a detailed history by historian Simon Lilley and engineer John Wenyon.

Using primary source material plus the records of such worthy individuals as Arthur Taylor, this joint authorship examines the rational for the building and operation of these engines from their appearance through to their demise.

Facts, figures and technical information abound as well as some fascinating records of the problems encountered in service both technical and operational.

Softcover, 108 pages
ISBN 978909328358 £16.50

Available at all good book shops, rail enthusiast shops, museums and preserved railways.
Crecy Publishing Ltd
1a Ringway Trading Est, Shadowmoss Rd, Manchester M22 5LH
Tel +44 (0)161 499 0024
www.crecy.co.uk

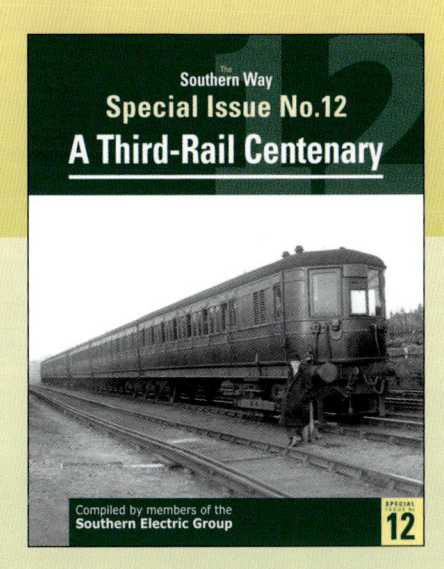

Southern Way Special Issue No 12
A Third-Rail Centenary
Paul Cooper

- Southern Way Special Issue No 12 is an extra edition for 2015 to celebrate a special anniversary
- Compiled by recognised experts from the 'Southern Electric Group'
- The authors proceeds will be directed towards the continued preservation of 4COR set No 3142

October 2015 sees the centenary of the start of third-rail electric services from Waterloo, an electric system that would develop over the years so much so that with the obvious exception of the 1940's there would continue to be expansion of the third-rail in every decade through to the 1960's – and even afterwards there would continue to be some additions later. Electrification was a new venture for the London & South Western Railway, a necessary change in order to combat the growing competition from some of the already established London lines and its neighbour the London, Brighton & South Coast Railway. What is so remarkable is that notwithstanding the difficulties of war, the new electrified lines were ready to start operation in the midst of conflict and would prove to be an immediate success. Here is the story of those early days, the stock of the time and even contemporary recollections of the reliability (or otherwise) of some of the first trains

Softcover, 120 pages, over 120 photographs
ISBN 9781909328396 £16.50

Available at all good book shops, rail enthusiast shops, museums and preserved railways.
Crecy Publishing Ltd
1a Ringway Trading Est, Shadowmoss Rd, Manchester M22 5LH
Tel +44 (0)161 499 0024
www.crecy.co.uk

The Southern Way

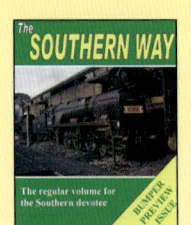

The regular volume for the Southern devotee
MOST RECENT BACK ISSUES

The Southern Way is available from all good book sellers, or in case of difficulty, direct from the publisher. (Post free UK) Each regular issue contains at least 96 pages including colour content.

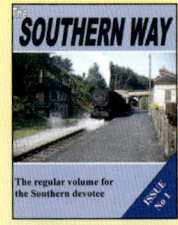

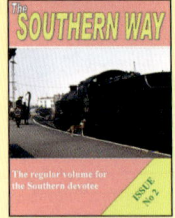

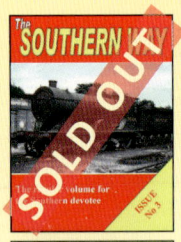

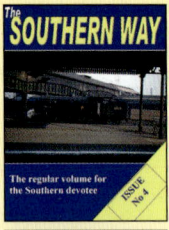

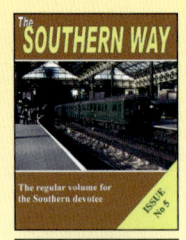

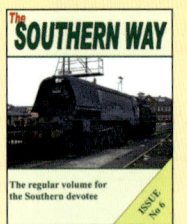

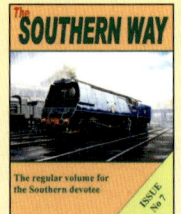

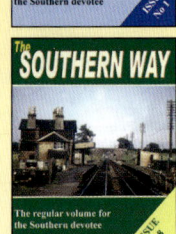

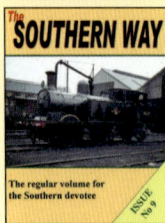

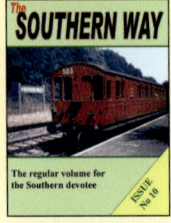

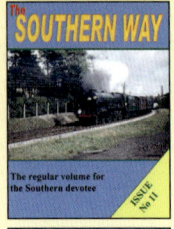

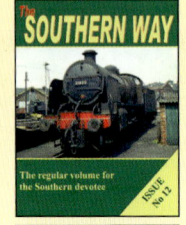

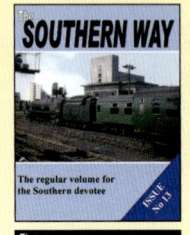

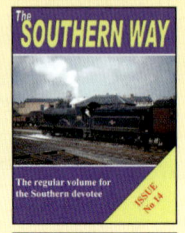

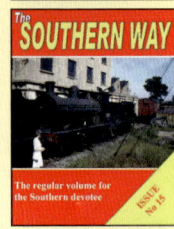

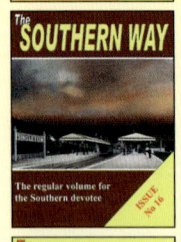

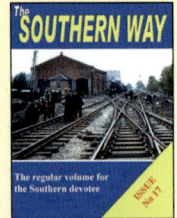

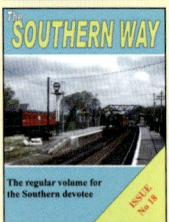

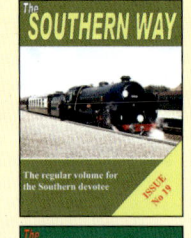

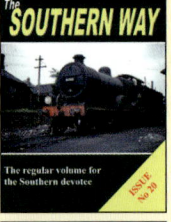

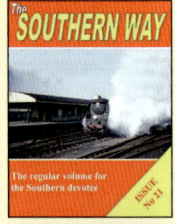

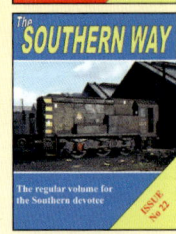

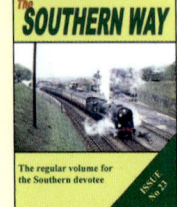

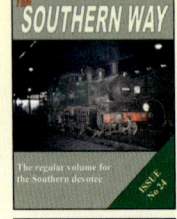

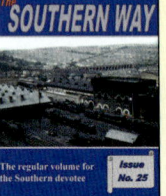

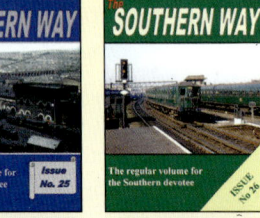

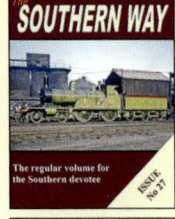

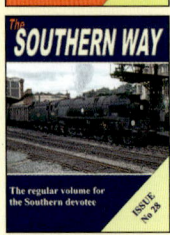

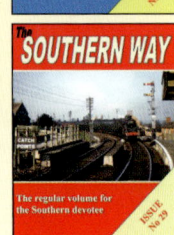

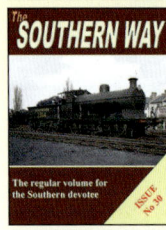

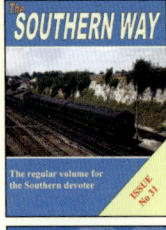

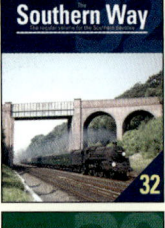

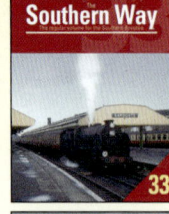

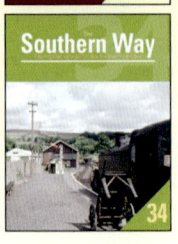

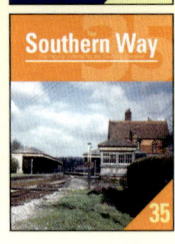

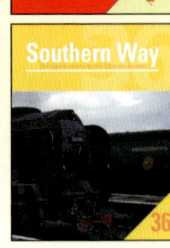

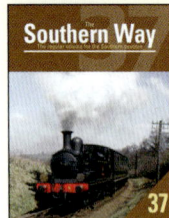

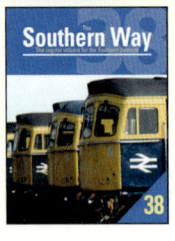

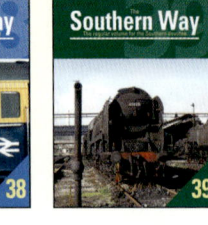

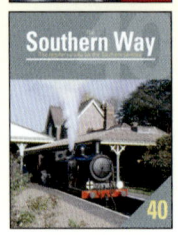

£11.95 each
£12.95 from Issue 7
£14.50 from Issue 21
£14.95 from Issue 35

Subscription for four-issues available
(Post free in the UK)
www.crecy.co.uk

120